CONSTITUTION

TO

CRISIS

DALE WALKER

Published in the United States of America

ISBN 978-1-955243-34-6 (SC)
ISBN 978-1-955243-35-3 (Ebook)

Dr. Dale Walker
222 West 6th Street
Suite 400, San Pedro, CA, 90731
http://constitutiontocrisis.com

Order Information and Rights Permission:

Quantity sales. Special discounts might be available on quantity purchases by corporations, associations, and others. For details, contact the publisher at the address above.

For Book Rights Adaptation and other Rights Permission. Call us at toll-free 1-888-945-8513 or send us an email at admin@stellarliterary.com.

DEDICATION

To my wonderful wife, Linda, for enduring the six years of struggles for my doctorate and the many hours in my office writing this book.

To my adult children, Scott, Kelly, and Doug for their support and encouragement, and to my grandchildren for their smiles and hugs for Pop.

To the guys at the coffee shop for their continued amazement at my accomplishments.

FOREWORD

This book describes the federal budget in a manner that is readable, and hopefully, understandable. The government's previous attempts at transparency and accountability have failed. Government reports may be transparent (you have access to them), but I challenge you to understand the terminology contained in the financial reports of the many bureaus of the government.

This book is ideal for students in government classes (graduate and undergraduate studies), anyone interested in learning more about the budget, the deficit, and opportunities to cut some of the 4000+ programs included in the budgets for the 20+ government bureaus. U.S. congressmen and women could benefit from this book if they would show a genuine interest in reducing spending without increasing taxes.

As you will see, there are many opportunities for eliminating programs.

What if.....

The federal budget for FY 2016 was based on the appropriate sections of the U.S. Constitution of 1787?

The federal budget was balanced using the U.S. Constitution?

The excess receipts remaining after the budget is balanced were distributed to the states?

The excess receipts were distributed to the states based on their population in accordance with the 'general welfare' clause of the Constitution?

The distribution to the states was to fund the federal bureaus that were dissolved and best run by the states?

The budget information in the following chapters is presented in tables to facilitate readability and understanding. The format presents the federal budget in sufficient detail to promote understanding of the programs within each department, within each agency, within each bureau.

INTRODUCTION

The purpose of the federal budget is to provide information to members of Congress, interested citizens, and students for understanding the impact of increasing tax revenues, increasing spending above tax revenues, and the cause for concern over budget deficits and the continued increases in the federal debt. The important ratio discussed is the ratio of the federal debt to the Gross Domestic Product (GDP). This ratio is similar to the debt ratio calculated by corporations to determine leverage for increased borrowing and the degree of risk involved in further borrowing.

Sections of this book will address the list of agencies and bureaus. Certain agencies, bureaus, and individual programs will be isolated because they appear to be excessive and unnecessary. Tables will summarize the budget information in a 'picture' rather than terms and definitions to enhance understanding of this complex subject.

The budget for fiscal year 2014 is presented in a financial format known as the Statement of Cash Flow. The U.S. government's annual audited financial statements are required to contain this statement in a format similar to the one that is required for corporate financial reports. At the present time, the government's Statement of Cash Flow is called the Statement of Changes in Cash Balance. The statement is unreadable and not in compliance with its own standards.

The format for financial reporting for corporations is controlled by Generally Accepted Accounting Principles (GAAP) and by the Federal Accounting Standards Advisory Board for all government entity reporting. The Statement of Cash Flow in this book complies with GAAP and the FASAB regulations for reporting the results of operations and the cash flow generated by operating activities, investing activities, and financing activities.

For purposes of illustration, operating activities in the federal budget will include all the bureaus that are mainly concerned with the overall operation of the government and the operation of the individual states. The selection of the bureaus included is subjective and, therefore, could be in error. The selection of the bureaus to be included in investing activities will contain those bureaus spending funds on infrastructure, housing, the space program, and military installations. Financing activities will only include the activity within the federal debt; the payment of principal and interest, and additional borrowing to finance deficit spending.

Each chapter will include the fiscal year 2014 budget for each of the federal bureaus. The agency budget will be included in a table for readability with explanations and questions to increase understanding.

GOVERNMENT MANDATE FOR CHANGE

The federal government is mandated by the Financial Accounting Standards Advisory Board (FASAB) to comply with all Statements of Federal Financial Accounting Standards (SFFAS). In particular, SFFAS Standard No. 24 details the elements to be contained in the federal consolidated financial report. Included in these elements is the Statement of Changes in Cash Balance which is intended to reflect the Generally Accepted Accounting Principles (GAAP) version of the Statement of Cash Flow.

As will be seen in Chapters 7 and 8, the federal budget is constructed according to the GAAP version of the Statement of Cash Flow statement in an effort to comply with SFFAS 24 and government regulations for reporting cash flow.

The purpose of the Statement of Cash Flow using the federal budget is to improve readability, and hopefully, understanding. An effort is made to identify budget activities that are operational (operating activities), activities that are long-term investments (investing activities), and activities that are debt related (financing activities). Some elements of the budget are 'grossed up' to provide a better understanding (interest on the federal debt).

CONTENTS

CHAPTER 1

HISTORICAL TIMELINE FOR GOVERNMENT BUREAUS

(1787 to 2016)

Constitution

The timeline begins with the preparation and approval of the U.S. Constitution in 1787 to the present time.

The timeline contains the basic departments assumed to be proposed in the Preamble and the Constitution and continues through the 1800s, 1900s, and the last department created in 2002 as a response to the attack in New York in 2001.

At the present time there are 20 government departments, 8 (assumed) original departments (including the District of Columbia) and 12 departments added between 1849 and 2002. Each of the 20 departments contains multiple bureaus to promote the objectives of the departments. There are 74 bureaus within the 8 original departments, and 145 bureaus within the other 12 departments.

The proposed budget for FY2016 includes 1937 programs for the 325 bureaus operating within the 124 agencies.

Original Structure 1789

(Based on author's interpretation of the Preamble and Articles of the U.S. Constitution of 1787)

- Executive Branch (currently has 12 bureaus)
- Legislative Branch (currently has 13 bureaus)
- Judicial Branch (currently has 9 bureaus)
- Department of War (currently has 11 bureaus)
- Department of Justice (currently has 12 bureaus)
- Department of the Treasury (currently has 10 bureaus)
- Department of State (currently has 5 bureaus)
- District of Columbia (currently has 2 bureaus)

Total of 8 departments in the original structure that now include 74 bureaus

Subsequent Departments (1849 to Present)

- Department of the Interior 1849 (17 bureaus) President Zachary Taylor
- Department of Agriculture 1889 (27 bureaus) President Benjamin Harrison

- Department of Commerce 1913 (13 bureaus) President Woodrow Wilson
- Department of Labor 1913 (13 bureaus) (previously in the Department of Commerce) President Woodrow Wilson
- Department of Veterans Affairs 1930 (4 bureaus) President Herbert Hoover
- Department of Health and Human Services 1953 (14 bureaus) President Dwight D. Eisenhower
- Department of Housing and Urban Development 1965 (10 bureaus) President Lyndon Johnson
- Department of Transportation 1966 (15 bureaus) President Lyndon Johnson
- Department of Energy 1977 (6 bureaus) President Jimmy Carter
- Department of Education 1979 (11 bureaus) President Jimmy Carter
- Environmental Protection Agency 1990 (1 bureau) President George HW Bush
- Department of Homeland Security 2002 (14 bureaus) President George W Bush

Total of 12 departments added since 1789 that now include 145 bureaus

There is a separate listing for the numerous miscellaneous bureaus, bureaus, and corporations in the following pages.

According to USA.gov, there are 479 government departments, agencies, and bureaus.

Selected Articles of the Constitution of the United States

Article I	Section 1.	All legislative Powers herein granted shall be vested in a Congress of the United States, which shall consist of a Senate and House of Representatives
		Senate
		House of Representatives
	Section 8.	Powers Granted to Congress
	[1]	The Congress shall have Power to lay and collect Taxes, Duties, Imposts and Excises, to pay the Debts and provide for the common Defence and general Welfare of the United States; but all Duties, Imposts, and Excises shall be uniform throughout the United States;
		Department of Defence (Defense)
		Income taxes, duties, imports, and excise taxes
	[2]	To borrow money on the credit of the United States;
		Department of the Treasury (Federal Debt Only)
	[3]	To regulate Commerce with foreign Nations, and among the several States, and with the Indian Tribes;
		Department of Commerce
	[4]	To establish a uniform Rule of Naturalization, and uniform Laws on the subject of Bankruptcies throughout the United States;
		Department of Justice
	[5]	To coin Money, regulate the Value thereof, and of foreign Coin, and fix the Standard of Weights and Measures;
		Department of the Treasury
	[6]	To provide for the Punishment of counterfeiting the Securities and current Coin of the United States;

		Secret Service Department of Justice
	[7]	To establish Post Offices and post Roads; Post Office
	[8]	To promote the Progress of Science and useful Arts, by securing for limited Times To Authors and Inventors the exclusive Right to their respective Writings and Discoveries; United States Copyright Office (Dept. of the Library of Congress)
	[9]	To constitute Tribunals inferior to the supreme Court; Department of Justice
	[10]	To define and punish Piracies and Felonies committed on the high Seas, and Offenses Against the Law of Nations; Department of Defence (Defense) Department of Justice International Affairs
	[11]	To declare War, grant Letters of Marque and Reprisal, and make Rules concerning Captures on Land and Water; Department of the Army Department of the Navy
	[12]	To raise and support Armies, but no Appropriation of Money to that Use shall be for a longer Term than two Years; Department of the Army
	[13]	To provide and maintain a Navy; Department of the Navy
	[14]	To make Rules for the Government and Regulation of the land and naval Forces; Department of Defence (Defense)
	[15]	To provide for calling forth the Militia to execute the Laws of the Union, suppress Insurrections and repel Invasions; Department of Defence (Defense)
	[16]	To provide for organizing, arming, and disciplining the Militia, and for governing such Part of them as may be employed in the Service of the United States, reserving to the States respectively, the Appointment of the Officers, and the Authority of training the Militia according to the discipline prescribed by Congress;

		Department of Defence (Defense)
	[17]	To establish the District of Columbia (shorten version) District of Columbia
	[18]	To make all Laws which shall be necessary and proper for carrying into Execution the foregoing Powers, and all other Powers vested by this Constitution in the Government of the United States, or in any Department or Officer thereof. Senate House of Representatives
Article II	Section 1.	The Executive Branch
	[1]	The executive Power shall be vested in a President of the United States of America. He Shall hold his Office during the Term of four Years, and, together with the Vice-President, Chosen for the same Term, be elected 9 (as follows). Executive Branch

Original Departments

Department of War (1789) (Defense, 1949)
Established 1789 by President George Washington

Mission Statement

The mission of the Department of Defense (DoD) is to provide the military forces needed to deter war and to protect the security of our country. The department's headquarters is at the Pentagon.

The mission of Defense.gov is to support the overall mission of the Department of Defense by providing official, timely and accurate information about defense policies, organizations, functions and operations. Also, Defense.gov is the single, unified starting point for finding military information online.

This mission is consistent with the DoD Principles of Information, which outline the Department's policy for providing information to military members, DoD civilians, military family members, the American public, the Congress, and the news media. The information you find here is cleared for public release in accordance with applicable DoD policies. (Dept. of Defense, 2015)

Date Established

On this date (August 7, 1789), President George Washington signed into law a bill that established the U.S. War Department. The measure had moved through the First Federal Congress (1789–1791) with relatively little controversy. With Jonathan Trumbull, Jr., of Connecticut presiding over the Committee of the Whole, the House debated the authorization bill in late June 1789. Pro-

Administration Representative Egbert Benson of New York introduced an amendment to include a phrase to the effect that the War Department Secretary would be "removable by the President," echoing language that had been included in a much more rancorous debate a few days earlier about the duties and powers of the proposed Secretary of Foreign Affairs (later the Secretary of State). Roger Sherman of Connecticut and John Page of Virginia opposed Benson's amendment, but it carried narrowly, 24 to 22. The entire bill passed the House easily on June 27, with little debate in an unrecorded vote. Soon thereafter, the Senate passed the bill. In choosing the department's first secretary, President Washington preferred continuity. He nominated Henry Knox—a key aide during the American Revolution and, since 1785, the secretary of war under the Articles of Confederation. (Dept. of Defense, 2015)

Department of Defense Constitution to Crisis

Bureaus included in original budget of 1789:

National Military Establishment (Combined military forces)

Bureaus included in current proposed budget of FY2016:

Department of Defense – Military Programs
Military Personnel
Operation and Maintenance
International Reconstruction and Other Assistance
Procurement
Research, Development, Test, and Evaluation
Military Construction
Family Housing
Revolving and Management Funds
Allowances
Trust Funds

Budget Increases during the Obama Administration

2009 – 7%	increase over 2008	budget
2010 – 5%	increase over 2009	budget
2011 – 11%	increase over 2010	budget
2012 – 4%	decrease over 2011	budget
2013 – 8%	decrease over 2012	budget
2014 – 2%	decrease over 2013	budget
2015 – 1%	increase over 2014	budget
2016 – 1%	increase over 2015	budget

Original Departments

Department of Justice
Established 1789 by President George Washington

Mission Statement

To enforce the law and defend the interests of the United States according to the law, to ensure public safety against threats foreign and domestic, to provide federal leadership in preventing and controlling crime, to seek just punishment for those guilty of unlawful behavior, and to ensure fair and impartial administration of justice for all Americans. (Dept. of Justice, 2015)

Date Established

The Department of Justice (DOJ) is a cabinet-level agency responsible for enforcing the laws of the United States federal government. DOJ ensures public safety against foreign and domestic threats, including terrorism, and preventing crime. The department includes such venerable law enforcement bureaus as the Federal Bureau of Investigation (FBI), US Marshals, the Bureau of Alcohol, Tobacco and Firearms (ATF) and the Drug Enforcement Administration (DEA). DOJ is led by the United States Attorney General, the nation's top law enforcement official and chief legal adviser to the President. Another top DOJ official is the Solicitor General, who represents the federal government in cases heard before the US Supreme Court. In spite of its mandate to enforce the law, Justice Department officials have been accused at times of bending or breaking the law to suit the political whims of an administration. This has been especially true during the current reign of President George W. Bush, whose attorneys general and solicitors general have been deeply involved with extralegal aspects of the Global War on Terrorism campaign. (Dept. of Justice, 2015)

Department of Justice
Constitution to Crisis

Bureaus included in original budget of 1789:
Department of Justice

Bureaus included in current proposed budget of FY2016:
Department of Justice
Radiation Exposure Compensation
Federal Bureau of Investigation
Legal Activities and U.S. Marshals
General Administration
United States Parole Commission
Interagency Law Enforcement
Drug Enforcement Administration
National Security Division
Bureau of Alcohol, Tobacco, Firearms, and Explosives
Office of Justice Programs
Federal Prison System

Budget Increases during the Obama Administration

2009 – 4%	increase over 2008	budget
2010 – 7%	increase over 2009	budget
2011 – 13%	increase over 2010	budget
2012 – 1%	decrease over 2011	budget
2013 – 1%	increase over 2012	budget
2014 – 4%	decrease over 2013	budget
2015 – 1%	decrease over 2014	budget
2016 – 7%	increase over 2015	budget

Original Departments
Department of the Treasury
Established 1789 by President George Washington

Mission Statement

Maintain a strong economy and create economic and job opportunities by promoting the conditions that enable economic growth and stability at home and abroad, strengthen national security by combating threats and protecting the integrity of the financial system, and manage the U.S. Government's finances and resources effectively. (Dept. of the Treasury, 2015)

Date Established

On September 2, 1789, Congress established a "Department of Treasury" to manage the new federal government's finances, and created the position of Secretary of the Treasury to run the new department. President George Washington appointed Alexander Hamilton as the first Secretary of the Treasury, taking office on September 11, 1789. Hamilton had served as George Washington's aide-de-camp during the Revolution and was a key player in the ratification of the US Constitution. Hamilton was viewed as a good choice for the treasury because of his financial and managerial acumen, which was needed to solve the problem of the new nation's heavy war debt.

Hamilton's first official act was to submit a report to Congress in which he laid the foundation for the nation's financial health. He surprised many members of Congress when he insisted that the country repay its war debt of $75 million dollar-for-dollar in order to establish a sound level of credit for the fledgling federal government. (Dept. of the Treasury, 2015)

Department of the Treasury
Constitution to Crisis

Bureaus included in original budget of 1789

Department of the Treasury (included the First Bank of the United States in 1791)

Bureaus included in current proposed budget for FY2016

Department of the Treasury
Departmental Offices
Financial Crimes Enforcement Network
Financial Management Service
Federal Financing Bank
Alcohol and Tobacco Tax and Trade Bureau
Bureau of Engraving and Printing
United States Mint
Bureau of the Public Debt
Internal Revenue Service
Comptroller of the Currency
Office of Thrift Supervision
Interest on the Public Debt

Budget Growth during the Obama Administration

2009 – 28%	increase over 2008	budget
2010 – 37%	decrease over 2009	budget
2011 – 20%	increase over 2010	budget
2012 – 6%	increase over 2011	budget
2013 – 10%	increase over 2012	budget
2014 – 17%	increase over 2013	budget
2015 – 15%	increase over 2014	budget
2016 – 11%	increase over 2015	budget

Original Departments
Department of State
Established 1789 by President George Washington

Mission Statement

Shape and sustain a peaceful, prosperous, just, and democratic world and foster conditions for stability and progress for the benefit of the American people and people everywhere. (Dept. of State, 2015)

Date Established

In July 1789, Congress and President George Washington approved legislation establishing a Department of Foreign Affairs, making it the first federal agency to be created under the new Constitution. In September of that same year, additional legislation changed the name to the Department of State and assigned to it a variety of domestic duties, including managing the US Mint, taking the census and maintaining the Great Seal of the United States. Most of the domestic duties were eventually turned over to other federal departments and bureaus during the 19th century, putting the State Department primarily in charge of foreign affairs.

The nation's first Secretary of State was Thomas Jefferson, appointed by President Washington on September 29, 1789. Despite this duty as the nation's top diplomat, Jefferson preferred a more inward or domestic perspective on how the United States should move forward—that is, focusing on the unexplored continent rather than becoming involved in developments in Europe. Those who agreed with Jefferson's philosophy came to be known as "Jeffersonians." The Federalists, led by Secretary of the Treasury Alexander Hamilton, supported the development of a strong international commerce and the creation of a navy capable of protecting US merchant vessels. (Dept. of State, 2015)

Department of State
Constitution to Crisis

Bureaus included in original budget of 1789:

Department of Foreign Affairs

Bureaus included in current proposed budget for FY2016:

Administration of Foreign Affairs
International Organizations and Conferences
International Commissions
Other – Foreign information and exchange activities
Other – Conduct of foreign affairs
Other - International development and humanitarian assistance
Other - Other advancement of commerce

Budget Growth in Obama Administration

2009 – 22%	increase over 2008	budget
2010 – 11%	increase over 2009	budget
2011 – 21%	increase over 2010	budget
2012 – 12%	increase over 2011	budget
2013 – 2%	decrease over 2012	budget
2014 – 4%	decrease over 2013	budget
2015 – 4%	decrease over 2014	budget
2016 – 0%	increase over 2015	budget

Departments Established in the 1800s
Department of the Interior
Date Established 1849

Mission Statement

The U.S. Department of the Interior protects America's natural resources and heritage, honors our cultures and tribal communities, and supplies the energy to power our future. (Dept. of the Interior, 2015)

Date Established

In 1789 Congress created three Executive Departments: Foreign Affairs (later in the same year renamed State), Treasury, and War. It also provided for an Attorney General and a Postmaster General. Domestic matters were apportioned by Congress among these departments.

The idea of setting up a separate department to handle domestic matters was put forward on numerous occasions. It wasn't until March 3, 1849, the last day of the 30th Congress that a bill was passed to create the Department of the Interior to take charge of the Nation's internal affairs.

The Interior Department had a wide range of responsibilities entrusted to it: the construction of the national capital's water system, the colonization of freed slaves in Haiti, exploration of western wilderness, oversight of the District of Columbia jail, regulation of territorial governments, management of hospitals and universities, management of public parks, and the basic responsibilities for Indians, public lands, patents, and pensions. In one way or another all of these had to do with the internal development of the Nation or the welfare of its people. (Dept. of the Interior, 2015)

Department of the Interior
Constitution to Crisis

Bureaus included in original budget of 1849

General Land Office
Indian Affairs
Part of Department of Defense
Part of Department of State

Bureaus included in the current proposed budget for FY2016

Department of the Interior
Bureau of Reclamation
Central Utah Project
Bureau of Land Management
Bureau of Ocean Energy Management, Regulation and Enforcement
Office of Surface Mining Reclamation and Enforcement
United States Fish and Wildlife Service
Bureau of Indian Affairs and Bureau of Indian Education
Department-Wide Programs
National Park Service
United States Geological Survey
Departmental Offices
Office of the Solicitor
Insular Affairs
Office of the Special Trustee for American Indians
National Indian Gaming Commission

Budget Growth during the Obama Administration

2009 – 20%	increase over the 2008	budget
2010 – 12%	increase over the 2009	budget

2011 – 1%	decrease over the 2010	budget
2012 – 6%	increase over the 2011	budget
2013 – 8%	decrease over the 2012	budget
2014 – 4%	decrease over the 2013	budget
2015 – 2%	decrease over the 2014	budget
2016 – 1%	increase over the 2015	budget

Departments Established in the 1800s
Department of the Agriculture
Date Established 1889

Mission Statement

We provide leadership on food, agriculture, natural resources, rural development, nutrition, and related issues based on sound public policy, the best available science, and efficient management.

Date Established

Be It Enacted by the Senate and House of Representatives of the United States of America in Congress assembled, That there is hereby established at the seat of government of the United States a Department of Agriculture, the general designs and duties of which shall be to acquire and to diffuse among the people of the United States useful information on subjects connected with agriculture in the most general and comprehensive sense of that word, and to procure, propagate, and distribute among the people new and valuable seeds and plants.

Thirty-Seventh Congress of the United States at the second session Begun and Held at the City of Washington in the District of Columbia. Galusha A. Grow, Speaker of the House of Representatives. Solomon Foot, President of the Senate pro tempore. Abraham Lincoln, President. Approved, May 15, 1862. (www.usda.gov)

Department of Agriculture
Constitution to Crisis

Bureaus included in original budget of 1889:

Salaries and Miscellaneous

Bureaus included in current proposed budget for FY2016:

Foreign Agricultural Service
Department of Agriculture
National Institute of Food and Agriculture
Rural Utilities Service
Natural Resources Conservation Service
Farm Service Agency
Forest Service
Departmental Management
Risk Management Agency
Office of the Secretary
Office of Communications
Office of the Inspector General
Office of Chief Economist
Office of the General Counsel
National Appeals Division
Economic Research Service
National Agricultural Statistics Service
Agricultural Research Service
Animal and Plant Health Inspection Service
Food Safety and Inspection Service
Grain Inspection, Packers and Stockyards Administration
Agricultural Marketing Service
Rural Housing Service
Rural Business Cooperative Service

Rural Development
Food and Nutrition Service

Budget Increases during the Obama Administration

2009 – 26%	increase over 2008	budget
2010 – 13%	increase over 2009	budget
2011 – 17%	increase over 2010	budget
2012 – 5%	decrease over 2011	budget
2013 – 1%	increase over 2012	budget
2014 – 6%	decrease over 2013	budget
2015 – 6%	decrease over 2014	budget
2016 – 2%	decrease over 2015	budget

Departments Established in the 1900s
Department of Commerce
Date Established 1913

Mission Statement

The U.S. Department of Commerce promotes job creation, economic growth, sustainable development and improved standards of living for all Americans by working in partnership with businesses, universities, communities and our nation's workers. The department touches the daily lives of the American people in many ways, with a wide range of responsibilities in the areas of trade, economic development, technology, entrepreneurship and business development, environmental stewardship, and statistical research and analysis.

To drive U.S. competitiveness in the global marketplace, the Commerce Department works to strengthen the international economic position of the United States and facilitates global trade by opening up new markets for U.S. goods and services. Here at home, the Commerce Department promotes progressive business policies that help America's businesses and entrepreneurs and their communities grow and succeed. Cutting-edge science and technology at the department fosters innovation, and a focus on research and development that moves quickly from the lab to the marketplace generates progress and new 21st century opportunities. No matter where businesses are in their life cycle, whether just getting off the ground or looking to expand into overseas markets, the Commerce Department is singularly focused on making U.S. companies more innovative at home and more competitive abroad, so they can create jobs.

The Commerce Department also provides effective management and monitoring of our nation's resources and assets to support both environmental and economic health. Through critical weather monitoring, weather forecasts and resource preservation, the department protects not only public safety and security but also our oceans, coasts and marine life while assisting their economic development. Other essential operations conducted by the Commerce Department include the constitutionally mandated decennial census, which serves as the basis of America's representative democracy, as well as the system by which businesses and innovators secure intellectual property rights. The Secretary of Commerce leads the department's efforts, overseeing a $7.5 billion budget and nearly 47,000 employees worldwide. (Dept. of Commerce, 2015)

Department of Commerce
Constitution to Crisis

Bureaus included in original budget of 1913:

Office of the Secretary
Bureau of Corporations
Bureau of Foreign and Domestic Commerce
Bureau of Navigation
Bureau of Standards
Bureau of Census
Coast and Geodetic Survey
Bureau of Lighthouses
Bureau of Fisheries
Steamboat-Inspection Service
Miscellaneous

Bureaus included in current proposed budget for FY2016:

Bureau of Industry and Security
National Oceanic and Atmospheric Administration
Department of Commerce
Departmental Management
Bureau of the Census
Economic and Statistical Analysis
International Trade Administration
Minority Business Development Agency
U.S. Patent and Trademark Office
National Institute of Standards and Technology
National Telecommunications and Information Administration
Economic Development Administration

Budget Growth during the Obama Administration

2009 – 39%	increase over the 2008	budget
2010 – 23%	increase over the 2009	budget
2011 – 10%	decrease over the 2010	budget
2012 – 11%	increase over the 2011	budget
2013 – 16%	decrease over the 2012	budget
2014 – 3%	decrease over the 2013	budget
2015 – 0%	increase over the 2014	budget
2016 – 2%	increase over the 2015	budget

Departments Established in the 1900s
Department of Labor
Established 1913 by President Woodrow Wilson

Mission Statement

To foster, promote, and develop the welfare of the wage earners, job seekers, and retirees of the United States; improve working conditions; advance opportunities for profitable employment; and assure work-related benefits and rights. (Dept. of Labor, 2015)

Date Established

The bill establishing the Department of Labor was signed on March 4, 1913, by President William Howard Taft, the defeated and departing incumbent just hours before Woodrow Wilson took office. Although Taft had misgivings about creating a new Cabinet-level Department, he realized that the new Congress and new President would surely reenact it if he did apply a veto. A Federal Department was the direct product of a half-century campaign by organized labor for a "Voice in the Cabinet." Also, the Department was an indirect product of the Progressive Movement of the early 1900s which promoted the achievement of better working conditions, conservation of natural resources and a host of other goals through both private and government action.

In the words of the organic act establishing the Department of Labor, its main purpose is "to foster, promote and develop the welfare of working people, to improve their working conditions, and to advance their opportunities for profitable employment." Economic and social conditions have changed constantly since 1913 and new statutory responsibilities have greatly expanded the Department's scope and mission. The succinct statement in the organic act remains, however, as the vital core of the Department's activities and the measuring rod against which its accomplishments should be gauged. (Dept. of Labor, 2015)

Department of Labor
Constitution to Crisis

Bureaus included in the original budget of 1913

Office of the Secretary
Bureau of Labor Statistics
Bureau of Immigration and Naturalization
Children's Bureau
Miscellaneous

Bureaus included in the current proposed budget for FY2016:

Office of Workers' Compensation Programs
Department of Labor
Employment and Training Administration
Departmental Management
Office of the American Workplace
Wage and Hour Division
Employment Standards Administration
Office of Federal Contract Compliance Programs
Office of Labor Management Standards
Occupational Safety and Health Administration
Mine Safety and Health Administration
Employee Benefits Security Administration
Pension Benefit Guaranty Corporation

Budget Increases during the Obama Administration

2009 – 135%	increase over 2008	budget
2010 – 25%	increase over 2009	budget
2011 – 14%	decrease over 2010	budget

2012 – 26%	decrease over 2011	budget
2013 – 24%	decrease over 2012	budget
2014 – 8%	decrease over 2013	budget
2015 – 6%	decrease over 2014	budget
2016 – 3%	decrease over 2015	budget

Departments Established in the 1900s
Department of Veterans Affairs
Established 1930 by President Herbert Hoover

Mission Statement

To fulfill President Lincoln's promise "To care for him who shall have borne the battle, and for his widow, and his orphan" by serving and honoring the men and women who are America's Veterans. (Dept. of Veterans Affairs, 2015)

Date Established

The federal government's first attempts at dispensing benefits to soldiers came during the Revolutionary War. During another war, the War of 1812, the government established the first federal facility for veterans at the Naval Home in Philadelphia. This was followed by two more facilities in Washington, DC: the Soldiers' Home in 1853 and St. Elizabeth's Hospital in 1855. In the meantime, US officials established the first administrative unit dedicated to helping veterans: the Bureau of Pensions in 1833.

During the 19th century, government officials expanded benefits and pensions not only for veterans, but also their spouses and dependents. By the end of the Mexican War in 1848, American veterans numbered in the hundreds of thousands. This number ballooned following the conclusion of the Civil War; there were approximately 1.9 million Union Army veterans on the federal rolls. Almost the same number existed in the Confederacy. However, Confederate veterans were not granted benefits by the federal government until 1958, for those still living. (Dept. of Veterans Affairs, 2015)

Department of Veterans Affairs
Constitution to Crisis

Bureaus included in original budget of 1930:

Veterans Health Administration
Department of Veterans Affairs
Benefits Programs
Departmental Administration

Bureaus included in current proposed budget of FY2016:

Department of Veterans Affairs
Veterans Health Administration
Benefits Programs
Departmental Administration

Budget Growth during the Obama Administration

2009 – 13%	increase over the 2008	budget
2010 – 13%	increase over the 2009	budget
2011 – 30%	increase over the 2010	budget
2012 – 12%	decrease over the 2011	budget
2013 – 8%	increase over the 2012	budget
2014 – 6%	increase over the 2013	budget
2015 – 5%	increase over the 2014	budget
2016 – 9%	increase over the 2015	budget

Departments Established in the 1900s
Department of Health and Human Services
Date Established 1953

Mission Statement

The U.S. Department of Health and Human Services (HHS) is the U.S. government's principal agency for protecting the health of all Americans and providing essential human services, especially for those who are least able to help themselves.

HHS is responsible for almost a quarter of all federal outlays and administers more grant dollars than all other federal bureaus combined. (Dept. of Health and Human Services, 2015)

Date Established

Before the federal government established a cabinet-level department to address health issues, lawmakers took a number of steps to create programs and bureaus that focused on health-related research and regulation. The earliest effort came in 1798 with the passage of an act to help sick and disabled seamen. This led to the establishment of a federal network of hospitals for the care of merchant seamen, forerunner of today's Public Health Service.

During the administration of President Abraham Lincoln, the Bureau of Chemistry was created within the Department of Agriculture. This move represented the earliest attempt to address food-related issues, and it helped lead to the founding of the Food and Drug Administration several decades later.

The post-Civil War era would see the appointment of the first Supervising Surgeon (later called Surgeon General) in 1871 for the Marine Hospital Service; the opening of a one-room laboratory on Staten Island for research on disease (the forerunner to the National Institutes of Health); and passage in 1891 of legislation that made the Marine Hospital Service responsible for medical examination of arriving immigrants.

Shortly after the turn of the 20th Century, the Public Health Service was officially established in 1902, and four years later, Congress passed the Pure Food and Drugs Act authorizing the government to monitor the purity of foods and the safety of medicines (another key step that led to the founding of the FDA). (Dept. of Health and Human Services, 2015)

Department of Health and Human Services
Constitution to Crisis

Bureaus included in original budget of 1953
Originally established as the Department of Health, Education, and Welfare

Bureaus included in current proposed budget for FY2016:
Centers for Disease Control and Prevention
Department of Health and Human Services
Administration for Children and Families
Health Resources and Services Administration
Indian Health Services
Substance Abuse and Mental Health Services Administration
Centers for Medicare and Medicaid Services
Administration on Aging
Departmental Management
Program Support Center
Office of the Inspector General
National Institutes of Health
Agency for Healthcare Research and Quality
Food and Drug Administration

Budget Growth during the Obama Administration

2009 – 14%	increase over the 2008	budget
2010 – 7%	increase over the 2009	budget
2011 – 7%	increase over the 2010	budget
2012 – 2%	decrease over the 2011	budget
2013 – 6%	increase over the 2012	budget
2014 – 14%	increase over the 2013	budget
2015 – 7%	increase over the 2014	budget
2016 – 8%	increase over the 2015	budget

Departments Established in the 1900s
Department of Housing and Urban Development
Established 1965

Mission Statement

HUD's mission is to create strong, sustainable, inclusive communities and quality affordable homes for all. HUD is working to strengthen the housing market to bolster the economy and protect consumers; meet the need for quality affordable rental homes; utilize housing as a platform for improving quality of life; build inclusive and sustainable communities free from discrimination, and transform the way HUD does business. (Dept. of Housing and Urban Development, 2015)

Date Established

Congress created the Federal Housing Administration (FHA) in 1934 to help Americans with their housing needs during the Great Depression.

In July 1947, the Housing and Home Finance Agency was established to help people buy homes following World War II. Two years later, the Housing Act of 1949 was enacted to help eradicate slums and promote redevelopment in urban areas.

Throughout the 1950s, FHA focused on broadening its mission. In September 1959, a new Housing Act allowed funds for elderly housing.

FHA became a part of the new Department of Housing and Urban Development created in September 1965. In the 1960s, HUD sought to eliminate discrimination through the implementation of the Fair Housing Act of 1968. The department also enforced the provisions of the Brooke Amendment in 1969, which established that low-income families would pay no more than 25% of their incomes for rent. Robert C. Weaver, HUD's first secretary, oversaw the department's anti-discrimination efforts under the Fair Housing Act—efforts that became especially important when riots broke out in predominantly African-American areas after the assassination of Dr. Martin Luther King, Jr. in 1968. The decade ended with the establishment of the Government National Mortgage Association (Ginnie Mae), which expanded availability of mortgage funds for moderate-income families. The government, using mortgage-backed securities, guaranteed these funds... (Dept. Housing and Urban Development, 2015)

Department of Housing and Urban Development
Constitution to Crisis

Bureaus included in original budget of 1962:

Department of Housing and Urban Development
Public and Indian Housing Programs
Housing Programs
Government National Mortgage Association
Community Planning and Development
Policy Development and Research
Management and Administration

Bureaus included in current proposed budget for FY2016:

Housing Programs
Department of Housing and Urban Development
Public and Indian Housing Programs
Government National Mortgage Association
Community Planning and Development
Policy Development and Research
Office of Lead Hazard Control and Healthy Homes
Management and Administration
Office of Sustainable Housing and Communities
Fair Housing and Equal Opportunity

Budget Growth during the Obama Administration

2009 – 24%	increase over the 2008	budget
2010 – 1%	decrease over the 2009	budget
2011 – 1%	increase over the 2010	budget

2012 – 19%	decrease over the 2011	budget
2013 – 8%	decrease over the 2012	budget
2014 – 4%	decrease over the 2013	budget
2015 – 4%	decrease over the 2014	budget
2016 – 1%	decrease over the 2015	budget

Departments Established in the 1900s
Department of Transportation
Established 1966 by President Lyndon Johnson

Mission Statement

Serve the United States by ensuring a fast, safe, efficient, accessible and convenient transportation system that meets our vital national interests and enhances the quality of life of the American people, today and into the future. (Dept. of Transportation, 2015)

Date Established

It was Najeeb Halaby, administrator of the independent Federal Aviation Agency, who proposed the idea of a cabinet-level Department of Transportation to President Lyndon Johnson's aides in 1965. Frustrated by the Defense Department's infringement upon certain transportation issues, such as supersonic transport, Halaby wanted to elevate transportation policy to a higher level. Halaby argued that the new department should assume the functions then under the authority of the undersecretary of commerce for transportation. Moreover, he recommended that the Federal Aviation Agency become part of that department.

Halaby got help from Charles Schultze, director of the Bureau of the Budget, and Joseph A. Califano, Jr., special assistant to the president, who together pushed for the new department. They urged the undersecretary of commerce for transportation to explore the prospects of having a transportation department initiative prepared as part of Johnson's 1966 legislative program. This launched the Boyd Task Force, which recommended the creation of a Department of Transportation that would include the Federal Aviation Agency, the Bureau of Public Roads, the Coast Guard, the Saint Lawrence Seaway Development Corporation, the Great Lakes Pilotage Association, the Car Service Division of the Interstate Commerce Commission, the subsidy function of the Civil Aeronautics Board, and the Panama Canal.

President Johnson agreed to the plan and sent it to Congress on March 6, 1966. It took considerable negotiation with lawmakers to get them to agree to approve the legislation, but finally, on October 15, 1966, the President was given the authority to create the Department of Transportation (DOT). (Dept. of Transportation, 2015)

Department of Transportation
Constitution to Crisis

Bureaus included in original budget of 1966:

Department of Transportation
Federal Highway Administration
Federal Railroad Administration
Federal Transit Administration
Federal Aviation Administration
Saint Lawrence Seaway Development Corporation
Maritime Administration
Office of the Secretary

Bureaus included in current proposed budget for FY2016:

Maritime Administration
Department of Transportation
National Infrastructure Bank
Office of the Secretary
Federal Highway Administration
Federal Motor Carrier Safety Administration
National Highway Traffic Safety Administration
Federal Railroad Administration
Federal Transit Administration
Surface Transportation Board
Saint Lawrence Seaway Development Corporation
Pipeline and Hazardous Materials Safety Administration
Research and Innovative Technology Administration
Office of Inspector General

Budget Growth during the Obama Administration

2009 – 12%	increase over the 2008	Budget
2010 – 7%	increase over the 2009	Budget
2011 – 2%	increase over the 2010	Budget
2012 – 13%	increase over the 2011	Budget
2013 – 6%	increase over the 2012	Budget
2014 – 3%	increase over the 2013	Budget
2015 – 2%	increase over the 2014	Budget
2016 – 3%	increase over the 2015	Budget

Departments Established in the 1900s
Department of Energy
Established 1977 by President Jimmy Carter

Mission Statement

The mission of the Energy Department is to ensure America's security and prosperity by addressing its energy, environmental and nuclear challenges through transformative science and technology solutions. (Dept. of Energy, 2015)

Date Established

The Department of Energy Organization Act of 1977 created one the most interesting and diverse bureaus in the Federal government. Activated on October 1, 1977, the twelfth cabinet-level department brought together for the first time within one agency two programmatic traditions that had long coexisted within the Federal establishment: 1) defense responsibilities that included the design, construction, and testing of nuclear weapons dating from the Manhattan Project effort to build the atomic bomb, and 2) a loosely knit amalgamation of energy-related programs scattered throughout the Federal government. (Dept. of Energy, 2015)

Department of Energy Constitution to Crisis

Bureaus included in original budget of 1977:

Environmental and Other Defense Activities
Energy Programs
Department of Energy
Power Marketing Administration
Departmental Administration

Bureaus included in current proposed budget for FY2016:

National Nuclear Security Administration
Environmental and Other Defense Activities
Department of Energy
Energy Programs
Power Marketing Administration
Departmental Administration

Budget Growth during the Obama Administration

2009 – 11%	increase over the 2008	budget
2010 – 30%	increase over the 2009	budget
2011 – 45%	increase over the 2010	budget
2012 – 7%	decrease over the 2011	budget
2013 – 16%	decrease over the 2012	budget
2014 – 10%	decrease over the 2013	budget
2015 – 3%	decrease over the 2014	budget
2016 – 6%	decrease over the 2015	budget

Departments Established in the 1900s
Department of Education
Date Established 1979 by President Jimmy Carter

Mission Statement

ED's mission is to promote student achievement and preparation for global competitiveness by fostering educational excellence and ensuring equal access. (Dept. of Education, 2015)

Date Established

Congress established the U.S. Department of Education (ED) on May 4, 1980, in the Department of Education Organization Act (Public Law 96-88 of October 1979). Under this law, ED's mission is to:

Strengthen the Federal commitment to assuring access to equal educational opportunity for every individual;

Supplement and complement the efforts of states, the local school systems and other instrumentalities of the states, the private sector, public and private nonprofit educational research institutions, community-based organizations, parents, and students to improve the quality of education;

Encourage the increased involvement of the public, parents, and students in Federal education programs;

Promote improvements in the quality and usefulness of education through Federally supported research, evaluation, and sharing of information;

Improve the coordination of Federal education programs;

Improve the management of Federal education activities; and

Increase the accountability of Federal education programs to the President, the Congress, and the public. (Dept. of Education, 2015)

Department of Education
Constitution to Crisis

Bureaus included in original budget of 1979:

The Office of Education was previously included in the Dept. of Health, Education, and Welfare.
Office of Elementary and Secondary Education
Office of English Language Acquisition
Office of Special Education and Rehabilitative Services
Office of Vocational and Adult Education
Office of Postsecondary Education
Office of Federal Student Aid
Department of Education
Institute of Education Sciences
Departmental Management

Bureaus included in current proposed budget for FY2016:

Department of Education
Office of Elementary and Secondary Education
Office of Innovation and Improvement
Office of Safe and Drug-Free Schools
Office of English Language Acquisition
Office of Special Education and Rehabilitative Services
Office of Vocational and Adult Education
Office of Postsecondary Education
Office of Federal Student Aid
Institute of Education Sciences
Departmental Management

Budget Growth during the Obama Administration

2009 – 19%	decrease over the 2008	budget
2010 – 74%	increase over the 2009	budget
2011 – 15%	decrease over the 2010	budget
2012 – 11%	decrease over the 2011	budget
2013 – 5%	decrease over the 2012	budget
2014 – 4%	increase over the 2013	budget
2015 – 8%	increase over the 2014	budget
2016 – 7%	increase over the 2015	budget

Departments Established in the 1900s
Environmental Protection Agency
Established 1990 by President George H.W. Bush

Mission Statement

To strengthen the capacity of small communities throughout America to improve and protect the health of their people and the environment in which they live. (Environmental Protection Agency, 2015)

Date Established

President Theodore Roosevelt, who undertook a western camping trip with Muir in 1903, came to symbolize the campaign for conservation, which gained steadily in political popularity. During and after his Administration, the use and retention of natural resources became a preoccupation of government.

President Franklin Roosevelt's New Deal enacted a number of natural resource measures. The Soil Conservation Service, founded in 1935, applied scientific practices to reduce the erosion of agricultural land. The depletion of animal life received recognition in the passage of the 1937 Pittman-Robertson Act, establishing a fund for state fish and wildlife programs from the proceeds of federal taxes on hunting and fishing equipment. Most ambitious of all, the Tennessee Valley Authority erected nine dams and a string of massive generating stations. (Environmental Protection Agency, 2015)

Bureaus included in original budget of 1990:

Environmental Protection Agency

Bureaus included in current proposed budget for FY2016:

Environmental Protection Agency

Budget Growth during the Obama Administration

2009 – 2%	increase over the 2008	budget
2010 – 36%	increase over the 2009	budget
2011 – 1%	increase over the 2010	budget
2012 – 10%	decrease over the 2011	budget
2013 – 27%	decrease over the 2012	budget
2014 – 1%	increase over the 2013	budget
2015 – 4%	increase over the 2014	budget
2016 – 3%	increase over the 2015	budget

Departments Established in the 2000s
Department of Homeland Security
Established 2002 by President George W. Bush

Mission Statement

Missions include preventing terrorism and enhancing security; managing our borders; administering immigration laws; securing cyberspace; and ensuring disaster resilience. (Dept. of Homeland Security, 2015)

Date Established

The terrorist attacks on Sept. 11, 2001, prompted federal officials to examine how such an attack was allowed to occur. The post-9/11 debate eventually turned to how the federal government could prevent future attacks by terrorists. Exactly one month after the attacks, Sen. Joe Lieberman (D-CT) and Sen. Arlen Specter (R-PA) introduced legislation to create a Department of Homeland Security. The Bush administration rejected the idea, but Democratic members of the Senate continued to press it. Finally, in June 2002, more than seven months after the initial proposal, President Bush reversed his stand. The Homeland Security Act called for pulling together various federal bureaus and offices into the newly established Department of Homeland Security (DHS), led by the first Secretary of Homeland Security, Tom Ridge, former Republican governor of Pennsylvania.

In creating DHS, some bureaus maintained their name and missions, while others ceased to exist and their duties were distributed among new DHS units. For example, the US Customs Service, formerly part of the Treasury Department, was split into the US Customs and Border Protection (CBP) and the US Immigration and Customs Enforcement (ICE). Likewise, the Immigration and Naturalization Service, a Justice Department office, was divided into CBP and ICE, along with the US Citizenship and Immigration Service. Altogether, the missions of 22 federal offices were either shifted or folded into DHS. (Dept. of Homeland Security, 2015)

Department of Homeland Security
Constitution to Crisis

Bureaus included in original budget of 2002:

Supporting First Responders
Defending Against Biological Terrorism
Securing America's Borders
Using 21st Century Technology to Defend the Homeland
Aviation Security
Other Non-Department of Defense (DOD) Homeland Security
DOD Homeland Security (Outside Initiatives)

Bureaus included in current proposed budget for FY2016:

United States Coast Guard
National Protection and Programs Directorate
Federal Emergency Management Agency
Science and Technology
Department of Homeland Security
Customs and Border Protection
Transportation Security Administration
Departmental Management and Operations
Office of the Inspector General
United States Secret Service
Domestic Nuclear Detection Office

Budget Growth during the Obama Administration

2009 – 27%	increase over the 2008	budget

2010 – 14%	decrease over the 2009	budget
2011 – 8%	increase over the 2010	budget
2012 – 2%	decrease over the 2011	budget
2013 – 3%	decrease over the 2012	budget
2014 – 3%	decrease over the 2013	budget
2015 – 3%	increase over the 2014	budget
2016 – 3%	increase over the 2015	budget

CHAPTER 2

DETAIL ANALYSIS OF BUDGETS

FY2014

FY2015

FY2016

Budget Summary

Federal Budgets	2014	2015	2016
Legislative Branch	5,025,000,000	4,980,000,000	5,075,000,000
Judicial Branch	7,275,000,000	7,337,000,000	7,476,000,000
Department of Agriculture	136,675,000,000	128,855,000,000	126,903,000,000
Department of Commerce	10,672,000,000	10,633,000,000	10,822,000,000
Department of Defense - Military	637,550,000,000	644,077,000,000	651,447,000,000
Department of Health and Human Services	1,048,641,000,000	1,117,768,000,000	1,208,597,000,000
Department of the Interior	12,127,000,000	11,914,000,000	11,985,000,000
Department of Justice	31,083,000,000	30,673,000,000	32,869,000,000
Department of Labor	76,699,000,000	72,039,000,000	70,030,000,000
Department of State	30,649,000,000	29,561,000,000	29,538,000,000
Department of the Treasury	725,673,000,000	833,564,000,000	926,126,000,000
Social Security Administration	908,222,000,000	957,547,000,000	1,015,005,000,000
Department of Education	69,878,000,000	75,742,000,000	81,233,000,000
Department of Energy	31,027,000,000	29,976,000,000	28,060,000,000
Environmental Protection Agency	7,349,000,000	7,628,000,000	7,860,000,000
Department of Transportation	97,432,000,000	99,337,000,000	102,278,000,000
General Services Administration	860,000,000	747,000,000	647,000,000
Department of Homeland Security	44,428,000,000	45,837,000,000	47,297,000,000
Department of Housing and Urban Development	43,609,000,000	41,710,000,000	41,195,000,000

National Aeronautics and Space Administration	18,032,000,000	18,040,000,000	18,326,000,000
Office of Personnel Management	87,255,000,000	91,066,000,000	94,453,000,000
Small Business Administration	878,000,000	874,000,000	890,000,000
Department of Veterans Affairs	142,811,000,000	150,330,000,000	163,808,000,000
Executive Office of the President	549,000,000	549,000,000	561,000,000
Federal Drug Control Program	347,000,000	332,000,000	336,000,000
International Assistance Programs	23,728,000,000	25,317,000,000	27,166,000,000
Other Defense Civil Programs	59,160,000,000	60,645,000,000	67,051,000,000
Corp of Engineers-Civil Works	5,644,000,000	5,059,000,000	4,978,000,000
District of Columbia	898,000,000	899,000,000	902,000,000
Postal Service	(206,000,000)	(208,000,000)	(210,000,000)
Numerous Boards, Commissions, Other	9,846,000,000	11,456,000,000	13,543,000,000
Undistributed Offsetting Receipts	(296,675,000,000)	(324,511,000,000)	(328,441,000,000)
Total Budget	3,977,141,000,000	4,189,773,000,000	4,467,806,000,000

Agency Name – Social Security Administration
Bureau Name – Social Security Administration

Account Name	2014	2015	2016
Administrative Expenses, Recovery Act	99,000	0	0
Attorney Fees, Federal Disability Insurance Trust Fund	-29,000	-29,000	-30,000
FDI, Federal Payments to the FDI Trust Fund	-2,874,000	-3,163,000	-3,433,000
FDI, Tax Refund Offset	-47,000	-47,000	-47,000
Federal Disability Insurance Trust Fund	43,000	51,000	55,000
Federal Disability Insurance Trust Fund	3,319,000	3,516,000	3,594,000
Federal Disability Insurance Trust Fund	144,990,000	149,656,000	154,610,000
Federal Old-age and Survivors Insurance Trust Fund	3,085,000	3,102,000	3,168,000
Federal Old-age and Survivors Insurance Trust Fund	701,435,000	744,447,000	790,675,000
FOASI, Attorney Fees	-1,000	-1,000	-1,000
FOASI, Federal Payments to the FOASI Trust Fund	-31,864,000	-35,584,000	-39,152,000
FOASI, Non-Attorney Fees	-1,000	-1,000	-1,000
FOASI, Tax Refund Offset	-16,000	-16,000	-16,000
Limitation on Administrative Expenses	118,000	0	0
Office of the Inspector General	-2,000	-1,000	0
Office of the Inspector General	29,000	29,000	30,000
Payments to Social Security Trust Funds	34,741,000	38,750,000	42,588,000
Receipts from SSI Administrative Fee	-158,000	-160,000	-175,000

Recovery of Beneficiary Overpayments from SSI Program	-3,588,000	-3,699,000	-3,810,000
Special Benefits for Certain World War II Veterans	1,000	1,000	1,000
Special Benefits for Certain World War II Veterans	6,000	5,000	5,000
SSI, Attorney Fees	-8,000	-8,000	-8,000
State Supplemental Fees	157,000	158,000	161,000
State Supplemental Fees, SSI	-194,000	-203,000	-231,000
Supplemental Security Income Program	3,767,000	3,812,000	3,914,000
Supplemental Security Income Program	55,214,000	56,932,000	63,108,000
Total	908,222,000	957,547,000	1,015,005,000

Agency Name – Small Business Administration
Bureau Name – Small Business Administration

Account Name	2014	2015	2016
Business Loan Fund Liquidating Account	-1,000,000	0	0
Business Loans Program Account	348,000,000	350,000,000	359,000,000
Disaster Loans Program Account	160,000,000	161,000,000	165,000,000
Office of Advocacy	9,000,000	9,000,000	9,000,000
Office of Inspector General	18,000,000	18,000,000	18,000,000
Salaries and Expenses	344,000,000	336,000,000	339,000,000
Total	878,000,000	874,000,000	890,000,000

Agency Name – Office of Personnel Management
Bureau Name – Office of Personnel Management

Account Name	2014	2015	2016
All Other General Fund Proprietary Receipts Including Budget Clearing Accounts	-2,000,000	-2,000,000	-2,000,000
Civil Service Retirement and Disability Fund	98,000,000	99,000,000	101,000,000
Civil Service Retirement and Disability Fund	80,955,000,000	84,209,000,000	87,543,000,000
Earnings on Investments, Postal Service Retiree Health Benefits Fund	-1,932,000,000	-2,266,000,000	-2,965,000,000
Employees and Retired Employees Health Benefits Funds	-431,000,000	-398,000,000	-586,000,000
Employees and Retired Employees Health Benefits Funds	51,000,000	52,000,000	54,000,000
Employees Life Insurance Fund	-1,876,000,000	-2,131,000,000	-2,303,000,000
Employees Life Insurance Fund	4,000,000	4,000,000	4,000,000
Flexible Benefits Plan Reserve	-1,000,000	0	-1,000,000
General Fund Payment to the Civil Service Retirement and Disability Fund	-35,078,000,000	-35,678,000,000	-36,678,000,000
Government Payment for Annuitants, Employee Life Insurance	49,000,000	51,000,000	53,000,000
Government Payment for Annuitants, Employees Health Benefits	12,391,000,000	13,324,000,000	14,337,000,000
Office of Inspector General	4,000,000	3,000,000	4,000,000
Payment to Civil Service Retirement and	35,078,000,000	35,678,000,000	36,678,000,000

Disability Fund			
Postal Service Contributions for Benefits Paid to Retirees, Postal Service Retiree Health Benefits Fund	-5,423,000,000	-5,573,000,000	-5,829,000,000
Postal Service Retiree Health Benefits Fund	3,329,000,000	3,657,000,000	4,004,000,000
Re-employed Annuitants Salary Offset, Civil Service Retirement and Disability Fund	-58,000,000	-59,000,000	-59,000,000
Salaries and Expenses	97,000,000	96,000,000	98,000,000
Total	87,255,000,000	91,066,000,000	94,453,000,000

Agency Name – National Aeronautical and Space Administration
Bureau Name – National Aeronautical and Space Administration

Account Name	2014	2015	2016
All Other General Fund Proprietary Receipts Including Budget Clearing Accounts	-15,000,000	-15,000,000	-15,000,000
Deltas between the Annualized CR Amounts and the FY 2011 Budget Request	-1,000,000	0	0
Working Capital Fund	0	-1,000,000	-2,000,000
Science, Space, and Technology Education Trust Fund	1,000,000	1,000,000	1,000,000
Office of Inspector General	37,000,000	37,000,000	38,000,000
Education	135,000,000	133,000,000	133,000,000
Construction, Environmental Compliance, and Remediation	439,000,000	435,000,000	436,000,000
Aeronautics	549,000,000	547,000,000	556,000,000
Space Technology	991,000,000	986,000,000	996,000,000
Cross Agency Support	3,070,000,000	3,082,000,000	3,141,000,000
Exploration	3,805,000,000	3,807,000,000	3,868,000,000
Space Operations	4,181,000,000	4,194,000,000	4,273,000,000
Science	4,840,000,000	4,834,000,000	4,901,000,000
Total	18,032,000,000	18,040,000,000	18,326,000,000

Agency Name – Judicial Branch

Bureau Name	Account Name	2014	2015	2016
Administrative Office of the United States Courts	Salaries and Expenses	85,000	86,000	88,000
Courts of Appeals, District Courts, and other Judicial Services	Registry Administration	2,000	3,000	3,000
Courts of Appeals, District Courts, and other Judicial Services	Fees of Jurors and Commissioners	57,000	58,000	59,000
Courts of Appeals, District Courts, and other Judicial Services	Judiciary Filing Fees	314,000	317,000	318,000
Courts of Appeals, District Courts, and other Judicial Services	Salaries and Expenses	353,000	353,000	353,000
Courts of Appeals, District Courts, and other Judicial Services	Judiciary Information Technology Fund	473,000	476,000	479,000
Courts of Appeals, District Courts, and other Judicial Services	Court Security	493,000	495,000	503,000
Courts of Appeals, District Courts, and other Judicial Services	Defender Services	1,056,000	1,062,000	1,086,000
Courts of Appeals, District Courts, and other Judicial Services	Salaries and Expenses	4,714,000	4,740,000	4,845,000
Federal Judicial Center	Salaries and Expenses	27,000	28,000	28,000

Judicial Branch	Advances and Reimbursements, Judiciary Information Technology Fund	-426,000	-413,000	-422,000
Judicial Branch	Proceeds from Sale of Property, Judiciary Information Technology Fund	-118,000	-121,000	-123,000
Judicial Branch	Federal Payment to Judicial Officers Retirement Fund	-106,000	-115,000	-127,000
Judicial Branch	Federal Payment to Judicial Survivors Annuities Fund	-13,000	-14,000	-14,000
Judicial Branch	Federal Payment to Claims Court Judges' Retirement Fund	-6,000	-6,000	-6,000
Judicial Retirement Funds	United States Court of Federal Claims Judges' Retirement Fund	4,000	4,000	4,000
Judicial Retirement Funds	Judicial Survivors' Annuities Fund	26,000	27,000	28,000
Judicial Retirement Funds	Judicial Officers' Retirement Fund	59,000	65,000	67,000
Judicial Retirement Funds	Payment to Judiciary Trust Funds	125,000	135,000	147,000
Supreme Court of the United States	Salaries and Expenses	3,000	3,000	3,000
Supreme Court of the United States	Care of the Building and Grounds	8,000	8,000	8,000
Supreme Court of the United States	Salaries and Expenses	71,000	71,000	73,000
United States Court of Appeals for the Federal Circuit	Salaries and Expenses	3,000	3,000	3,000

United States Court of Appeals for the Federal Circuit	Salaries and Expenses	31,000	32,000	32,000
United States Court of International Trade	Salaries and Expenses	2,000	2,000	2,000
United States Court of International Trade	Salaries and Expenses	20,000	20,000	21,000
United States Sentencing Commission	Salaries and Expenses	18,000	18,000	18,000
Total		7,275,000	7,337,000	7,476,000

Agency Name – International Assistance Programs

Bureau Name	Account Name	2014	2015	2016
African Development Foundation	Gifts and Donations, African Development Foundation	-3,000	-3,000	-3,000
African Development Foundation	Gifts and Donations, African Development Foundation	2,000	2,000	2,000
African Development Foundation	African Development Foundation	25,000	26,000	26,000
Agency for International Development	Economic Assistance Loans Liquidating Account	-241,000	-228,000	-226,000
Agency for International Development	Gifts and Donations, Agency for International Development	-20,000	-20,000	-20,000
Agency for International Development	Foreign Service National Separation Liability Trust Fund	-4,000	-4,000	-4,000
Agency for International Development	General Fund Proprietary Interest Receipts, not Otherwise Classified	-1,000	-1,000	-1,000
Agency for International Development	Foreign Service National Separation Liability Trust Fund	4,000	4,000	4,000
Agency for International Development	Assistance for the Independent States of the Former Soviet Union	7,000	4,000	3,000
Agency for International Development	Miscellaneous Trust Funds, AID	15,000	15,000	10,000

Bureau Name	Account Name	2014	2015	2016
Agency for International Development	Child Survival and Health Programs	16,000	9,000	6,000
Agency for International Development	Housing and Other Credit Guaranty Programs Liquidating Account	19,000	17,000	14,000
Agency for International Development	Transition Initiatives	53,000	57,000	59,000
Agency for International Development	Operating Expenses, Office of Inspector General	55,000	57,000	58,000
Agency for International Development	Development Credit Authority Program Account	68,000	77,000	66,000
Agency for International Development	HIV/AIDS Working Capital Fund	70,000	60,000	25,000
Agency for International Development	Capital Investment Fund of the United States Agency for International Development.	210,000	214,000	218,000
Agency for International Development	Assistance for Europe, Eurasia and Central Asia	668,000	675,000	663,000
Agency for International Development	International Disaster Assistance	833,000	890,000	927,000
Agency for International Development	Operating Expenses of the Agency for International Development	1,615,000	1,692,000	1,740,000
Agency for International Development	Development Assistance Program	2,672,000	2,841,000	2,992,000
Inter-American Foundation	Inter-American Foundation	20,000	20,000	20,000

Bureau Name	Account Name	2014	2015	2016
International Assistance Program	Deltas between the Annualized CR Amounts and the FY 2011 Budget Request	-235,000	-87,000	-67,000
International Assistance Program	Deltas between the Annualized CR Amounts and the FY 2011 Budget Request	665,000	531,000	333,000
International Security Assistance	Foreign Military Loan Liquidating Account	-145,000	-54,000	-41,000
International Security Assistance	Global Security Contingency Fund	53,000	54,000	55,000
International Security Assistance	Pakistan Counterinsurgency Capability Fund	55,000	0	0
International Security Assistance	International Military Education and Training	114,000	117,000	120,000

International Assistance Programs (Continued)

Bureau Name	Account Name	2014	2015	2016
International Security Assistance	Peacekeeping Operations	307,000	314,000	320,000
International Security Assistance	Nonproliferation, Antiterrorism, Demining, and Related Programs	735,000	754,000	770,000
International Security Assistance	Foreign Military Financing Program	5,822,000	5,956,000	6,087,000
International Security Assistance	Economic Support Fund	6,777,000	6,604,000	6,543,000
Military Sales Program	Deposits, Advances, Foreign Military Sales Trust Fund	-26,644,000	-25,312,000	-23,413,000
Military Sales Program	Foreign Military Sales Trust Fund	-43,000	0	0
Military Sales Program	Foreign Military Sales Trust Fund	25,166,000	24,662,000	24,280,000
Millennium Challenge Corporation	Millennium Challenge Corporation	818,000	1,100,000	1,249,000
Multilateral Assistance	Debt Restructuring	15,000	16,000	16,000
Multilateral Assistance	Contribution to Enterprise for the Americas Multilateral Investment Fund	19,000	24,000	26,000

Bureau Name	Account Name	2014	2015	2016
Multilateral Assistance	Contributions to the International Fund for Agricultural Development	24,000	31,000	32,000
Multilateral Assistance	International Affairs Technical Assistance Program	31,000	32,000	32,000
Multilateral Assistance	Contribution to the Inter-American Development Bank	129,000	132,000	135,000
Multilateral Assistance	Strategic Climate Fund	201,000	206,000	210,000
Multilateral Assistance	Contribution to the Asian Development Bank	222,000	223,000	234,000
Multilateral Assistance	Contribution to the African Development Bank	246,000	254,000	257,000
Multilateral Assistance	Contribution to the International Bank for Reconstruction and Development	277,000	283,000	288,000
Multilateral Assistance	Global Food Security Fund	327,000	333,000	340,000
Multilateral Assistance	International Organizations and Programs	369,000	377,000	384,000
Multilateral Assistance	Clean Technology Fund	424,000	433,000	442,000
Multilateral Assistance	Contribution to the International Development Association	1,615,000	1,649,000	1,682,000
Overseas Private Investment Corporation	Overseas Private Investment Corporation Noncredit Account	-202,000	-225,000	-241,000

Bureau Name	Account Name	2014	2015	2016
Overseas Private Investment Corporation	Overseas Private Investment Corporation Loans, Negative Subsidies	-96,000	-102,000	-105,000
Overseas Private Investment Corporation	Overseas Private Investment Corporation Program Account	61,000	62,000	62,000
Peace Corps	Host Country Resident Contractors Separation Liability Fund	1,000	1,000	1,000
Peace Corps	Peace Corps	464,000	474,000	484,000
Special Assistance Initiatives	Tsunami Recovery and Reconstruction Fund	5,000	0	0
Trade and Development Agency	Trade and Development Agency	68,000	71,000	72,000
Total		23,728,000	25,317,000	27,166,000

Agency Name – General Services Administration

Bureau Name	Account Name	2014	2015	2016
General Activities	Working Capital Fund	-1,000	-1,000	-2,000
General Activities	Allowances and Office Staff for Former Presidents	4,000	4,000	4,000
General Activities	Acquisition Workforce Training Fund	12,000	12,000	12,000
General Activities	Federal Acquisition Workforce Initiatives Fund	17,000	17,000	17,000
General Activities	Electronic Government (E-GOV) Fund	32,000	33,000	33,000
General Activities	Federal Citizen Services Fund	38,000	39,000	40,000
General Activities	Office of Inspector General	60,000	60,000	62,000
General Activities	Operating Expenses	66,000	67,000	68,000
General Activities	Government-wide Policy	101,000	101,000	103,000
General Services Administration	All Other General Fund Proprietary Receipts Including Budget Clearing Accounts	-26,000	-26,000	-26,000
General Services Administration	Recoveries of Transportation Charges	-13,000	-13,000	-13,000
General Services Administration	Other Receipts, Surplus Real and Related Personal Property	-12,000	-12,000	-12,000
General Services Administration	Acquisition Workforce Training Fund	-12,000	-12,000	-12,000
General Services Administration	Undistributed Intragovernmental Payments and Receivables from Cancelled Accounts	-11,000	-11,000	-11,000

General Services Administration	Land and Water Conservation Fund, Surplus Property Sales	-5,000	-5,000	-5,000
General Services Administration	Receipts of Rent, Leases and Lease Payments for Government Owned Real Property	-3,000	-3,000	-3,000
General Services Administration	Transfers of Surplus Real and Related Personal Property Receipts	5,000	5,000	5,000
Real Property Activities	Disposal of Surplus Real and Related Personal Property	9,000	9,000	9,000
Real Property Activities	Federal Buildings Fund	212,000	346,000	365,000
Real Property Activities	Federal Buildings Fund, Recovery Act	374,000	124,000	0
Supply and Technology Activities	Expenses of Transportation Audit Contracts and Contract Administration	13,000	13,000	13,000
Total		860,000	747,000	647,000

Agency Name – Executive Office of the President

Bureau Name	Account Name	2014	2015	2016
Council of Economic Advisers	Salaries and Expenses	4,000	4,000	4,000
Council on Environmental Quality and Office of Environmental Quality	Council on Environmental Quality and Office of Environmental Quality	2,000	2,000	3,000
Executive Residence at the White House	White House Repair and Restoration	1,000	1,000	1,000
Executive Residence at the White House	Operating Expenses	13,000	13,000	14,000
National Security Council and Homeland Security Council	Salaries and Expenses	13,000	13,000	13,000
Office of Administration	Salaries and Expenses	111,000	111,000	115,000
Office of Management and Budget	Office of Management and Budget	89,000	89,000	91,000
Office of National Drug Control Policy	Office of National Drug Control Policy	22,000	22,000	22,000
Office of Science and Technology Policy	Office of Science and Technology Policy	6,000	6,000	6,000
Office of the United States Trade Representative	Office of the United States Trade Representative	49,000	49,000	50,000
Special Assistance to the President and the Official Residence of the Vice President	Special Assistance to the President and the Official Residence of the Vice President	5,000	5,000	5,000
The White House	The White House	57,000	57,000	58,000
Unanticipated Needs	Partnership Fund for Program Integrity Innovation	19,000	19,000	20,000

Unanticipated Needs	Integrated, Efficient and Effective Uses of Information Technology	58,000	58,000	59,000
Unanticipated Needs	Spectrum Relocation Fund	100,000	100,000	100,000
Total		549,000	549,000	561,000

Agency Name – Environmental Protection Agency

Bureau Name	2014	2015	2016
Environmental Protection Agency	-2,000	-2,000	-2,000
Environmental Protection Agency	41,000	41,000	41,000
Environmental Protection Agency	-10,000	-11,000	-11,000
Environmental Protection Agency	-17,000	-12,000	-7,000
Environmental Protection Agency	2,767,000	2,751,000	2,809,000
Environmental Protection Agency	-32,000	-30,000	-30,000
Environmental Protection Agency	8,000	10,000	12,000
Environmental Protection Agency	197,000	192,000	194,000
Environmental Protection Agency	1,049,000	1,021,000	1,029,000
Environmental Protection Agency	24,000	22,000	23,000
Environmental Protection Agency	-1,016,000	-1,022,000	-1,046,000
Environmental Protection Agency	13,000	13,000	12,000
Environmental Protection Agency	95,000	97,000	98,000
Environmental Protection Agency	44,000	45,000	45,000
Environmental Protection Agency	1,016,000	1,022,000	1,046,000
Environmental Protection Agency	14,000	14,000	14,000
Environmental Protection Agency	-104,000	-104,000	-104,000
Environmental Protection Agency	-30,000	-35,000	-36,000
Environmental Protection Agency	-4,000	0	0
Environmental Protection Agency	-50,000	-52,000	-53,000
Environmental Protection Agency	770,000	796,000	804,000
Environmental Protection Agency	2,000	1,000	-1,000

Environmental Protection Agency	2,591,000	2,886,000	3,039,000
Environmental Protection Agency	-6,000	-4,000	-3,000
Environmental Protection Agency	-3,000	-3,000	-3,000
Environmental Protection Agency	-8,000	-8,000	-8,000
Environmental Protection Agency	0	0	-2,000
Total	7,349,000	7,628,000	7,860,000

Agency Name – District of Columbia

Bureau Name	Account Name	2014	2015	2016
District of Columbia General and Special Payments	Federal Contribution, DC Federal Pension Fund	-476,000	-483,000	-469,000
District of Columbia General and Special Payments	Earnings on Investments, DC Federal Pension Fund	-131,000	-142,000	-151,000
District of Columbia Courts	Federal Payments, D.C. Judicial Retirement and Survivors Annuity	-9,000	-10,000	-10,000
District of Columbia Courts	All Other General Fund Proprietary Receipts Including Budget Clearing Accounts	-1,000	-1,000	-1,000
District of Columbia Courts	Federal Payment to the District of Columbia Courts	0	-1,000	0
District of Columbia Courts	Federal Payment to the District of Columbia Judicial Retirement and Survivors Annuity Fund	9,000	10,000	10,000
District of Columbia Courts	District of Columbia Judicial Retirement and Survivors Annuity Fund	9,000	10,000	10,000
District of Columbia General and Special Payments	Federal Payment for Emergency Planning and Security Cost in the District of Columbia	14,000	14,000	15,000
District of Columbia General and Special Payments	Federal Payment for Resident Tuition Support	34,000	34,000	35,000
District of Columbia Courts	Defender Services in District of Columbia Courts	53,000	53,000	54,000

District of Columbia General and Special Payments	Federal Support for Economic Development and Management Reforms in the District	56,000	56,000	57,000
District of Columbia General and Special Payments	Federal Payment for School Improvement	63,000	64,000	65,000
District of Columbia Courts	Federal Payment to the District of Columbia Courts	227,000	227,000	224,000
District of Columbia General and Special Payments	Federal Payment to the District of Columbia Pension Fund	476,000	483,000	469,000
District of Columbia General and Special Payments	District of Columbia Federal Pension Fund	574,000	585,000	594,000
Total		898,000	899,000	902,000

Agency Name – Veterans Affairs

Bureau Name	Account Name	2014	2015	2016
Benefits Programs	Housing Liquidating Account	- 7,000	-6,000	-4,000
Benefits Programs	Service-disabled Veterans Insurance Fund	1,000	0	0
Benefits Programs	Native American Veteran Housing Loan Program Account	1,000	1,000	1,000
Benefits Programs	Native American Veteran Housing Loan Program Account	1,000	1,000	1,000
Benefits Programs	Post-Vietnam Era Veterans Education Account	1,000	1,000	1,000
Benefits Programs	United States Government Life Insurance Fund	3,000	2,000	2,000
Benefits Programs	Veterans Reopened Insurance Fund	29,000	28,000	26,000
Benefits Programs	Veterans Special Life Insurance Fund	73,000	87,000	99,000
Benefits Programs	Veterans Insurance and Indemnities	110,000	115,000	120,000
Benefits Programs	Veterans Housing Benefit Program Fund	164,000	170,000	175,000
Benefits Programs	Burial benefits	256,000	257,000	267,000
Benefits Programs	Veterans Housing Benefit Program Fund	566,000	629,000	695,000

Bureau Name	Account Name	2014	2015	2016
Benefits Programs	National Service Life Insurance Fund	1,031,000	971,000	916,000
Benefits Programs	Pensions benefits	5,692,000	6,324,000	7,711,000
Benefits Programs	Readjustment Benefits	12,024,000	12,493,000	13,085,000
Benefits Programs	Compensation	61,475,000	66,004,000	75,502,000
Department of Veterans Affairs	Third Party Collections, MCCF	-2,396,000	-2,374,000	-2,403,000
Department of Veterans Affairs	Pharmaceutical Co-payments, MCCF	-708,000	-766,000	-779,000
Department of Veterans Affairs	First Party Collections, MCCF	-167,000	-167,000	-167,000
Department of Veterans Affairs	Contributions from Military Personnel, Veteran's Educational Assistance Act of 1984	-110,000	-92,000	-73,000
Department of Veterans Affairs	NSLI Fund, Premium and Other Receipts	-62,000	-54,000	-44,000
Department of Veterans Affairs	Compensated Work Therapy, MCCF	-57,000	-57,000	-57,000
Department of Veterans Affairs	General Post Fund, National Homes, Deposits	-27,000	-27,000	-27,000
Department of Veterans Affairs	Housing Negative Subsidies	-14,000	-10,000	-8,000
Department of Veterans Affairs	General Fund Proprietary Interest Receipts, not Otherwise Classified	-7,000	-7,000	-7,000
Department of Veterans Affairs	Parking Fees, MCCF	-4,000	-4,000	-4,000
Department of Veterans Affairs	MCCF, Long-term Care Copayments	-3,000	-3,000	-3,000

Bureau Name	Account Name	2014	2015	2016
Department of Veterans Affairs	Enhanced-use Lease Proceeds, MCCF	-2,000	-2,000	-2,000
Department of Veterans Affairs	Payments from Compensation and Pension, MCCF	-2,000	-2,000	-2,000
Department of Veterans Affairs	Deltas between the Annualized CR Amounts and the FY 2011 Budget Request	-2,000	-1,000	-1,000
Department of Veterans Affairs	Native American Veteran Housing Loans, Negative Subsidies	-1,000	-1,000	-1,000
Department of Veterans Affairs	Contributions, Post-Vietnam Era Veterans Education Account	-1,000	-1,000	-1,000
Departmental Administration	Franchise Fund	-5,000	-5,000	-5,000
Departmental Administration	Grants for Construction of Veterans Cemeteries	-1,000	0	0
Departmental Administration	Grants for Construction of State Extended Care Facilities	0	-1,000	0
Departmental Administration	Grants for Construction of Veterans Cemeteries	35,000	36,000	37,000
Departmental Administration	Grants for Construction of State Extended Care Facilities	103,000	94,000	93,000
Departmental Administration	Office of Inspector General	112,000	116,000	119,000
Departmental Administration	National Cemetery Administration	260,000	268,000	276,000

Bureau Name	Account Name	2014	2015	2016
Departmental Administration	Construction, Minor Projects	567,000	579,000	591,000
Departmental Administration	Construction, Major Projects	818,000	746,000	687,000
Departmental Administration	General Operating Expenses	2,548,000	2,627,000	2,708,000
Departmental Administration	Information Technology Systems	3,300,000	3,400,000	3,507,000
Veterans Health Administration	DOD-VA Health Care Sharing Incentive Fund	8,000	0	0
Veterans Health Administration	General Post Fund, National Homes	39,000	39,000	39,000
Veterans Health Administration	Medical and Prosthetic Research	525,000	541,000	558,000
Veterans Health Administration	Medical Services	854,000	880,000	907,000
Veterans Health Administration	Medical Facilities	5,565,000	5,723,000	5,895,000
Veterans Health Administration	Medical Support and Compliance	5,877,000	6,058,000	6,243,000
Veterans Health Administration	Medical Services	44,349,000	45,720,000	47,135,000
Total		142,811,000	150,330,000	163,808,000

Agency Name - Transportation

Bureau Name	Account Name	2014	2015	2016
Department of Transportation	Pipeline Safety Fund	-90,000	-91,000	-93,000
Department of Transportation	Deltas between the Annualized CR Amounts and the FY 2011 Budget Request	-56,000	-37,000	-4,000
Department of Transportation	Advances from State Cooperating Agencies and Foreign Governments, FHA Miscellaneous Trust	-38,000	-38,000	-38,000
Department of Transportation	Hazardous Materials Transportation Registration, Filing, and Permit Fees, Emergency Preparedness Grants	-28,000	-28,000	-28,000
Department of Transportation	Hazardous Materials Approvals and Permits Fund	-12,000	-12,000	-12,000
Department of Transportation	Pipeline Safety Design Review Fund	-5,000	-5,000	-5,000
Department of Transportation	Hazardous Materials Transportation Registration, Filing, and Permit Fees, Administrative Costs	-1,000	-1,000	-1,000
Department of Transportation	Pipeline Safety Special Permit Fund	-1,000	-1,000	-1,000

Bureau Name	Account Name	2014	2015	2016
Department of Transportation	Advances from Other Federal Agencies, FHA Miscellaneous Trust	-1,000	-1,000	-1,000
Department of Transportation	Proprietary Receipts, Miscellaneous Trust Funds	-1,000	-1,000	-1,000
Federal Aviation Administration	Aviation Insurance Revolving Fund	-215,000	-236,000	-256,000
Federal Aviation Administration	Administrative Services Franchise Fund	3,000	-1,000	-4,000
Federal Aviation Administration	Facilities and Equipment	50,000	0	0
Federal Aviation Administration	Grants-in-aid for Airports (Airport and Airway Trust Fund)	123,000	121,000	117,000
Federal Aviation Administration	Research, Engineering and Development (Airport and Airway Trust Fund)	184,000	184,000	186,000
Federal Aviation Administration	Grants-in-aid for Airports	558,000	0	0
Federal Aviation Administration	Grants-in-aid for Airports (Airport and Airway Trust Fund)	2,449,000	2,388,000	2,236,000
Federal Aviation Administration	Facilities and Equipment (Airport and Airway Trust Fund)	2,954,000	2,783,000	2,802,000
Federal Aviation Administration	Operations	4,675,000	4,695,000	4,783,000
Federal Aviation Administration	Trust Fund Share of FAA Activities (Airport	4,761,000	4,791,000	4,902,000

Bureau Name	Account Name	2014	2015	2016
	and Airway Trust Fund)			
Federal Highway Administration	Right-of-way Revolving Fund Liquidating Account	0	-3,000	0
Federal Highway Administration	Federal-aid Highways	2,000	0	0
Federal Highway Administration	TIFIA General Fund Program Account, Federal Highway Administration, Transportation	4,000	4,000	4,000
Federal Highway Administration	Appalachian Development Highway System	8,000	4,000	1,000
Federal Highway Administration	Miscellaneous Transportation Trust Funds	13,000	6,000	3,000
Federal Highway Administration	Miscellaneous Appropriations	20,000	20,000	20,000
Federal Highway Administration	Miscellaneous Trust Funds	41,000	40,000	40,000
Federal Highway Administration	Miscellaneous Appropriations	116,000	90,000	54,000
Federal Highway Administration	Highway Infrastructure Programs	188,000	112,000	21,000
Federal Highway Administration	Highway Infrastructure Investment, Recovery Act	710,000	707,000	0
Federal Highway Administration	Federal-aid Highways	19,930,000	17,860,000	17,743,000

Bureau Name	Account Name	2014	2015	2016
Federal Highway Administration	Federal-aid Highways	32,389,000	35,726,000	38,067,000
Federal Motor Carrier Safety Administration	Motor Carrier Safety Grants	8,000	11,000	14,000
Federal Motor Carrier Safety Administration	Motor Carrier Safety Grants	355,000	379,000	410,000
Federal Motor Carrier Safety Administration	Motor Carrier Safety Operations and Programs	383,000	425,000	473,000
Federal Railroad Administration	Capital Assistance for High Speed Rail Corridors and Intercity Passenger Rail Service	-325,000	-383,000	-512,000
Federal Railroad Administration	Pennsylvania Station Redevelopment Project	7,000	6,000	0
Federal Railroad Administration	Railroad Research and Development	39,000	39,000	39,000
Federal Railroad Administration	Network Development	135,000	192,000	264,000
Federal Railroad Administration	Safety and Operations	138,000	140,000	141,000
Federal Railroad Administration	Capital Assistance for High- Speed Rail Corridors and Intercity Passenger Rail Service	181,000	240,000	210,000
Federal Railroad Administration	Capital Assistance for High- Speed Rail Corridors and Intercity Passenger Rail Service	329,000	388,000	516,000
Federal Railroad	Network Development	1,590,000	2,263,000	3,122,000

Bureau Name	Account Name	2014	2015	2016
Administration				
Federal Railroad Administration	Capital Assistance for High-Speed Rail Corridors and Intercity Passenger Rail Service	1,648,000	2,183,000	1,913,000
Federal Railroad Administration	System Preservation	2,821,000	2,194,000	2,082,000
Federal Transit Administration	Capital Investment Grants	-7,000	-3,000	50,000
Federal Transit Administration	Transit Formula Grants	-4,000	-6,000	-7,000
Federal Transit Administration	Job Access and Reverse Commute Grants	-2,000	0	0
Federal Transit Administration	Grants for Energy Efficiency and Greenhouse Gas Reductions	-1,000	-1,000	0
Federal Transit Administration	Washington Metropolitan Area Transit Authority	0	0	-1,000
Federal Transit Administration	Bus and Rail State of Good Repair	0	0	1,000
Federal Transit Administration	Capital Investment Grants	7,000	3,000	-49,000
Federal Transit Administration	Research and University Research Centers	8,000	4,000	0
Federal Transit Administration	Job Access and Reverse Commute Grants	11,000	2,000	0

Bureau Name	Account Name	2014	2015	2016
Federal Transit Administration	Discretionary Grants (Transportation Trust Fund, Mass Transit Account)	13,000	0	0
Federal Transit Administration	Fixed Guideway Infrastructure Investment, Recovery Act	23,000	0	0
Federal Transit Administration	Research and University Research Centers	26,000	12,000	0
Federal Transit Administration	Grants for Energy Efficiency and Greenhouse Gas Reductions	39,000	21,000	15,000
Federal Transit Administration	Operations and Safety	39,000	41,000	42,000
Federal Transit Administration	Transit Capital Assistance, Recovery Act	42,000	0	0
Federal Transit Administration	Research and Technology Deployment	50,000	33,000	17,000
Federal Transit Administration	Formula Grants	69,000	8,000	7,000
Federal Transit Administration	Washington Metropolitan Area Transit Authority	144,000	144,000	147,000
Federal Transit Administration	Operations and Safety	146,000	151,000	155,000
Federal Transit Administration	Transit Challenge Grants, Trust Fund	368,000	974,000	1,614,000

Bureau Name	Account Name	2014	2015	2016
Federal Transit Administration	Capital Investment Grants	410,000	318,000	95,000
Federal Transit Administration	Bus and Rail State of Good Repair	3,735,000	4,181,000	4,773,000
Federal Transit Administration	Transit Formula Grants	8,437,000	7,877,000	7,457,000
Maritime Administration	Vessel Operations Revolving Fund	-1,000	-1,000	-1,000
Maritime Administration	Ready Reserve Force	0	0	-1,000
Maritime Administration	Maritime Guaranteed Loan (title XI) Program Account	4,000	4,000	4,000
Maritime Administration	Ship Disposal	18,000	18,000	18,000
Maritime Administration	Operations and Training	155,000	155,000	158,000
Maritime Administration	Maritime Security Program	167,000	168,000	172,000
Maritime Administration	Ocean Freight Differential	175,000	175,000	175,000
National Highway Traffic Safety Administration	Highway Traffic Safety Grants	-2,000	0	0
National Highway Traffic Safety Administration	Operations and Research (Transportation Trust Fund)	0	0	-1,000
National Highway Traffic Safety Administration	Operations and Research	7,000	0	0

Bureau Name	Account Name	2014	2015	2016
National Highway Traffic Safety Administration	Highway Traffic Safety Grants	15,000	12,000	12,000
National Highway Traffic Safety Administration	Operations and Research (Transportation Trust Fund)	368,000	416,000	458,000
National Highway Traffic Safety Administration	Highway Traffic Safety Grants	697,000	769,000	858,000
National Infrastructure Bank	National Infrastructure Bank	2,121,000	2,618,000	2,906,000
Office of Inspector General	Salaries and Expenses	86,000	86,000	88,000
Office of the Secretary	Working Capital Fund	0	-1,000	-1,000
Office of the Secretary	Minority Business Resource Center Program	1,000	1,000	1,000
Office of the Secretary	Minority Business Outreach	3,000	3,000	3,000
Office of the Secretary	Office of Civil Rights	10,000	10,000	10,000
Office of the Secretary	Transportation Planning, Research, and Development	10,000	10,000	10,000
Office of the Secretary	Livable Communities	10,000	10,000	10,000
Office of the Secretary	Financial Management Capital	16,000	16,000	16,000
Office of the	Essential Air Service	50,000	50,000	50,000

Bureau Name	Account Name	2014	2015	2016
Secretary	and Rural Airport Improvement Fund			
Office of the Secretary	Supplemental Discretionary Grants for a National Surface Transportation System, Recovery Act	105,000	30,000	0
Office of the Secretary	Salaries and Expenses	113,000	113,000	115,000
Office of the Secretary	Payments to Air Carriers	118,000	118,000	121,000
Office of the Secretary	National Infrastructure Investments	860,000	502,000	272,000
Pipeline and Hazardous Materials Safety Administration	Operational Expenses	20,000	20,000	20,000
Pipeline and Hazardous Materials Safety Administration	Trust Fund Share of Pipeline Safety	21,000	21,000	22,000
Pipeline and Hazardous Materials Safety Administration	Emergency Preparedness Grants	28,000	28,000	28,000
Pipeline and Hazardous Materials Safety Administration	Pipeline Safety	34,000	35,000	36,000
Pipeline and Hazardous Materials Safety Administration	Hazardous Materials Safety	49,000	49,000	50,000

Bureau Name	Account Name	2014	2015	2016
Pipeline and Hazardous Materials Safety Administration	Pipeline Safety	60,000	62,000	61,000
Research and Innovative Technology Administration	Research and Development	18,000	18,000	18,000
Saint Lawrence Seaway Development Corporation	Operations and Maintenance	33,000	33,000	34,000
Surface Transportation Board	Salaries and Expenses	29,000	29,000	30,000
Total		97,432,000	99,337,000	102,278,000

Agency Name - Treasury

Bureau Name	Account Name	2014	2015	2016
Alcohol and Tobacco Tax and Trade Bureau	Salaries and Expenses	93,000	94,000	95,000
Alcohol and Tobacco Tax and Trade Bureau	Internal Revenue Collections for Puerto Rico	425,000	436,000	447,000
Bureau of the Public Debt	Payment of Government Losses in Shipment	1,000	1,000	1,000
Bureau of the Public Debt	Reimbursements to Federal Reserve Banks	130,000	132,000	134,000
Bureau of the Public Debt	Administering the Public Debt	159,000	160,000	163,000
Comptroller of the Currency	Assessment Funds	-44,000	-45,000	-46,000
Department of the Treasury	Interest Received from Credit Financing Accounts	-68,275,000	-71,167,000	-73,506,000
Department of the Treasury	Proceeds, GSE Equity Related Transactions	-16,738,000	-14,365,000	-10,610,000
Department of the Treasury	Interest on Loans to Federal Financing Bank	-4,094,000	-5,153,000	-5,335,000
Department of the Treasury	Interest on Loans and Repayable Advances to the Federal Unemployment Account	-1,720,000	-1,820,000	-1,720,000
Department of the Treasury	Charges for Administrative Expenses of Social Security Act As Amended	-1,050,000	-1,064,000	-1,078,000

Bureau Name	Account Name	2014	2015	2016
Department of the Treasury	Interest on Deposits in Tax and Loan Accounts	-1,048,000	-1,165,000	-1,189,000
Department of the Treasury	Interest on Loans to National Flood Insurance Fund, DHS	-757,000	-766,000	-867,000
Department of the Treasury	All Other General Fund Proprietary Receipts	-510,000	-510,000	-510,000
Department of the Treasury	Interest on Loans to BPA	-406,000	-469,000	-530,000
Department of the Treasury	Interest on Loans to Commodity Credit Corporation	-199,000	-220,000	-235,000
Department of the Treasury	Payment of Interest on Advances to the Railroad Retirement Board	-164,000	-185,000	-206,000
Department of the Treasury	Interest on Loans to the Helium Fund, Department of Interior	-158,000	-130,000	-127,000
Department of the Treasury	Interest on Loans to Temporary Corporate Credit Union Stabilization Fund, NCUA	-156,000	-129,000	-89,000
Department of the Treasury	New Installment Agreements, IRS Miscellaneous Retained Fees	-139,000	-139,000	-139,000
Department of the Treasury	Interest on Loans to Federal Deposit Insurance Corporation	-113,000	-189,000	-261,000
Department of the Treasury	Interest Payments on Repayable Advances to the Black Lung Disability Trust Fund	-82,000	-107,000	-134,000
Department of the Treasury	General User Fees, IRS Miscellaneous Retained Fees	-78,000	-78,000	-78,000
Department of the Treasury	Debt Collection	-78,000	-78,000	-78,000
Department of the Treasury	Underpayment and Fraud Collection	-50,000	-50,000	-50,000

Bureau Name	Account Name	2014	2015	2016
Department of the Treasury	Restructured Installment Agreements, IRS Miscellaneous Retained Fees	-36,000	-36,000	-36,000
Department of the Treasury	Troubled Asset Relief Program, Negative Subsidies	-32,000	0	0
Department of the Treasury	Interest on Quota in International Monetary Fund	-23,000	-23,000	-23,000
Department of the Treasury	Interest Payments from States, Cash Management Improvement	-21,000	-23,000	-26,000
Department of the Treasury	Reimbursement from Federal Agencies for Payments Made As a Result of Discriminatory Conduct	-10,000	-10,000	-10,000
Department of the Treasury	Interest on Investment, Colorado River Projects	-9,000	-9,000	-9,000
Department of the Treasury	General Fund Proprietary Interest Receipts, not Otherwise Classified	-5,000	-5,000	-5,000
Department of the Treasury	Gifts to the United States, not Otherwise Classified	-3,000	-3,000	-3,000
Department of the Treasury	Interest on Loans to the Presidio	-3,000	-3,000	-3,000
Department of the Treasury	Gifts to the United States for Reduction of the Public Debt	-3,000	-3,000	-3,000
Department of the Treasury	Interest on Loans for College Housing and Academic Facilities Loans, Education	-3,000	-2,000	-2,000
Department of the Treasury	Interest on Loans to the Secretary of Transportation, Ocean Freight Differential	-1,000	-1,000	-1,000

Bureau Name	Account Name	2014	2015	2016
Department of the Treasury	Earnings on Investments, Treasury Forfeiture Fund	-1,000	-1,000	-1,000
Department of the Treasury	Deltas between the Annualized CR Amounts and the FY 2011 Budget Request	1,000	0	0
Departmental Offices	Interest on Loans or Advances to the Extended Unemployment Compensation Account	-430,000	-440,000	-480,000
Departmental Offices	Exchange Stabilization Fund	-302,000	-307,000	-312,000
Departmental Offices	Treasury Franchise Fund	-2,000	-1,000	-2,000
Departmental Offices	Presidential Election Campaign Fund	0	37,000	113,000
Departmental Offices	Department-wide Systems and Capital Investments Programs	1,000	1,000	0
Departmental Offices	Working Capital Fund	2,000	0	0
Departmental Offices	State Small Business Credit Initiative	6,000	6,000	4,000
Departmental Offices	GSE Mortgage-Backed Securities Purchase Program Account	14,000	11,000	8,000
Departmental Offices	Office of Inspector General	30,000	29,000	29,000
Departmental Offices	Special Inspector General for the Troubled Asset Relief Program	45,000	45,000	46,000
Departmental Offices	Small Business Lending Fund Program Account	76,000	77,000	79,000
Departmental Offices	Financial Research Fund	93,000	95,000	97,000

Bureau Name	Account Name	2014	2015	2016
Departmental Offices	Treasury Inspector General for Tax Administration	151,000	152,000	155,000
Departmental Offices	Community Development Financial Institutions Fund Program Account	219,000	218,000	221,000
Departmental Offices	Office of Financial Stability	230,000	211,000	155,000
Departmental Offices	Salaries and Expenses	314,000	313,000	320,000
Departmental Offices	Treasury Forfeiture Fund	337,000	195,000	158,000
Departmental Offices	Terrorism Insurance Program	390,000	359,000	237,000
Departmental Offices	Treasury Forfeiture Fund	463,000	269,000	217,000
Departmental Offices	Grants for Specified Energy Property in Lieu of Tax Credits, Recovery Act	1,841,000	1,172,000	447,000
Departmental Offices	Troubled Asset Relief Program, Home Affordable Modification Program	5,134,000	4,109,000	2,083,000
Federal Financing Bank	Federal Financing Bank	-464,000	-200,000	-520,000
Financial Crimes Enforcement Network	Salaries and Expenses	109,000	109,000	111,000
Financial Management Service	Cheyenne River Sioux Tribe Terrestrial Wildlife Habitat Restoration Trust Fund	2,000	0	0
Financial Management	Federal Interest Liabilities to States	2,000	2,000	2,000

Bureau Name	Account Name	2014	2015	2016
Service				
Financial Management Service	Check Forgery Insurance Fund	2,000	2,000	2,000
Financial Management Service	Interest on Uninvested Funds	8,000	8,000	8,000
Financial Management Service	Salaries and Expenses	67,000	68,000	69,000
Financial Management Service	Salaries and Expenses	211,000	212,000	216,000
Financial Management Service	Federal Reserve Bank Reimbursement Fund	327,000	333,000	339,000
Financial Management Service	Financial Agent Services	618,000	625,000	631,000
Financial Management Service	Claims, Judgments, and Relief Acts	848,000	848,000	848,000
Financial Management Service	Payment to the Resolution Funding Corporation	2,628,000	2,628,000	2,628,000
Financial Management Service	Interest Paid to Credit Financing Accounts	20,118,000	20,003,000	19,529,000
Interest on the Public Debt	Interest Paid to Expenditure Accounts - Shadow Account	7,688,000	9,052,000	10,389,000
Interest on the Public Debt	Interest Paid to Federal Fund Receipt Accounts - Shadow	12,562,000	13,972,000	15,303,000

Bureau Name	Account Name	2014	2015	2016
	Account			
Interest on the Public Debt	Interest Paid to Trust Fund Receipt Accounts - Shadow Account	186,705,000	197,457,000	207,121,000
Interest on the Public Debt	Interest on Treasury Debt Securities (gross)	464,290,000	544,004,000	613,328,000
Internal Revenue Service	Health Insurance Tax Credit Administration	17,000	18,000	18,000
Internal Revenue Service	Payment to Issuer of Qualified Zone Academy Bonds	28,000	28,000	28,000
Internal Revenue Service	Payment to Issuer of New Clean Renewable Energy Bonds	28,000	28,000	28,000
Internal Revenue Service	Payment in Lieu of Tax Credit for Growth Zones	43,000	43,000	40,000
Internal Revenue Service	Informant Payments	50,000	50,000	50,000
Internal Revenue Service	Payment to Issuer of Qualified Energy Conservation Bonds	57,000	57,000	57,000
Internal Revenue Service	Payment Where Health Coverage Tax Credit Exceeds Liability for Tax	147,000	147,000	155,000
Internal Revenue Service	Business Systems Modernization	297,000	300,000	302,000
Internal Revenue Service	Payment Where Small Business Health Insurance Tax Credit Exceeds Liability for Tax	336,000	357,000	315,000
Internal Revenue Service	Enforcement	700,000	715,000	728,000
Internal Revenue Service	Payment to Issuer of Qualified School Construction Bonds	1,023,000	1,023,000	1,023,000

Bureau Name	Account Name	2014	2015	2016
Internal Revenue Service	Taxpayer Services	2,231,000	2,244,000	2,292,000
Internal Revenue Service	Refunding Internal Revenue Collections, Interest	3,778,000	3,928,000	4,179,000
Internal Revenue Service	Payment Where American Opportunity Credit Exceeds Liability for TAX	4,465,000	4,425,000	4,655,000
Internal Revenue Service	Operations Support	4,870,000	5,068,000	5,310,000
Internal Revenue Service	Build America Bond Payments, Recovery Act	5,578,000	6,731,000	7,895,000
Internal Revenue Service	Enforcement	5,949,000	6,362,000	6,844,000
Internal Revenue Service	Refundable Premium Assistance Tax Credit	15,585,000	32,023,000	42,645,000
Internal Revenue Service	Payment Where Child Tax Credit Exceeds Liability for Tax	25,509,000	25,586,000	25,587,000
Internal Revenue Service	Payment Where Earned Income Credit Exceeds Liability for Tax	45,860,000	45,893,000	46,477,000
Total		725,673,000	833,564,000	926,126,000

CHAPTER 3

FEDERAL BUDGET BASED ON THE PREAMBLE AND ARTICLES IN THE CONSTITUTION

CRISIS

This chapter presents the FY2016 federal budget in a format based on the departments mentioned in the Preamble and the Articles in the Constitution. It is presumed the budget for these departments is funded by an equal amount that covers all the department expenses and, therefore, results in a balanced budget (Constitutional Budget).

It is also presumed the excess receipts not used to balance the 'Constitutional Budget' are to be distributed to all the states according to population. The distribution to the states complies with the wording in the Preamble regarding 'promoting the general welfare'.

In other words, the distribution to each state is 'per capita' and implies the funds are to be used for 'all citizens' and not for any particular segment of the population in compliance with the 'general welfare' clause in the Preamble.

Construction of a Constitutional Budget

Constitutional Budget	FY2016		
Executive Branch - George Washington, 1789	561,000,000		
Legislative Branch - George Washington, 1789	5,075,000,000		
Judicial Branch - George Washington, 1789	7,476,000,000		
Department of War - George Washington, 1789	651,447,000,000		
Department of Justice - George Washington, 1789	32,869,000,000		
Department of the Treasury - George Washington, 1789	926,126,000,000		
Department of State - George Washington, 1789	29,538,000,000	1,653,092,000,000	100%
Added Since 1789		Cumulative	
Department of the Interior 1849 - President Zachary Taylor	11,985,000,000	1,665,077,000,000	
Department of Agriculture 1889 - President Benjamin Harrison	126,900,000,000	1,791,980,000,000	
Department of Commerce 1913 - President Woodrow Wilson	10,822,000,000	1,802,802,000,000	
Department of Labor 1913 - President Woodrow Wilson	70,030,000,000	1,872,832,000,000	
Department of Veterans Affairs 1930 - President Herbert Hoover	163,808,000,000	2,036,640,000,000	
Department of Health and Human Services 1953 - President Dwight D. Eisenhower	1,208,597,000,000	3,245,237,000,000	
Department of Housing and Urban Development 1965 - President Lyndon Johnson	41,195,000,000	3,286,432,000,000	

Department of Transportation 1966 - President Lyndon Johnson	102,278,000,000	3,388,700,000,000	
Department of Energy 1977 - President Jimmy Carter	28,060,000,000	3,416,760,000,000	
Department of Education 1979 - President Jimmy Carter	81,233,000,000	3,497,993,000,000	
Environmental Protection Agency 1990 - President George HW Bush	7,860,000,000	3,505,853,000,000	
Department of Homeland Security 2002 - President George W Bush	47,297,000,000	3,553,150,000,000	
Subtotal	3,553,150,000,000		
Numerous boards, commissions, and non-governmental organizations	914,656,000,000		
Total Budget	4,467,803,000,000	Percent Increase	170%

Distribution Table

The following table illustrates the amount of funds that would be directed to the states based on population for the 'general welfare' and not for a particular group.

Distribution of excess receipts based on population (promoting the general welfare) for FY2015:

State	Population	Distribution		State	Population	Distribution
Alabama	4,833,722	25,754,070,816		Missouri	6,044,171	32,203,343,088
Alaska	735,132	3,916,783,296		Montana	1,015,165	5,408,799,120
Arizona	6,626,624	35,306,652,672		Nebraska	1,868,516	9,955,453,248
Arkansas	2,959,373	15,767,539,344		Nevada	2,790,136	14,865,844,608
California	38,332,521	204,235,671,888		New Hampshire	1,323,459	7,051,389,552
Colorado	5,268,367	28,069,859,376		New Jersey	8,899,339	47,415,678,192
Connecticut	3,596,080	19,159,914,240		New Mexico	2,085,287	11,110,409,136
Delaware	925,749	4,932,390,672		New York	19,651,127	104,701,204,656
District of Columbia	646,449	3,444,280,272		North Carolina	9,848,060	52,470,463,680
Florida	19,552,860	104,177,638,080		North Dakota	723,393	3,854,237,904
Georgia	9,992,167	53,238,265,776		Ohio	11,570,808	61,649,265,024
Hawaii	1,404,054	7,480,799,712		Oklahoma	3,850,568	20,515,826,304
Idaho	1,612,136	8,589,460,608		Oregon	3,930,065	20,939,386,320
Illinois	12,882,135	68,636,015,280		Pennsylvania	12,773,801	68,058,811,728
Indiana	6,570,902	35,009,765,856		Rhode Island	1,051,511	5,602,450,608
Iowa	3,090,416	16,465,736,448		South Carolina	4,774,839	25,440,342,192

Kansas	2,893,957	15,419,002,896		South Dakota	844,877	4,501,504,656
Kentucky	4,395,295	23,418,131,760		Tennessee	6,495,978	34,610,570,784
Louisiana	4,625,470	24,644,504,160		Texas	26,448,193	140,915,972,304
Maine	1,328,302	7,077,193,056		Utah	2,900,872	15,455,846,016
Maryland	5,928,814	31,588,720,992		Vermont	626,630	3,338,684,640
Massachusetts	6,692,824	35,659,366,272		Virginia	8,260,405	44,011,437,840
Michigan	9,895,622	52,723,874,016		Washington	6,971,406	37,143,651,168
Minnesota	5,420,380	28,879,784,640		West Virginia	1,854,304	9,879,731,712
Mississippi	2,991,207	15,937,150,896		Wisconsin	5,742,713	30,597,174,864
				Wyoming	582,658	3,104,401,824
				Totals	316,128,83 9	1,684,333,000,000

Total Population as of 2013 is 316,128,839

Total Distributed is 1,684,333,000,000 for FY2015 ($5,328 per capita)

The District of Columbia is included with the States

Budget based on the United States Constitution of 1787

Preamble to the United States Constitution

We, the people of the United States, in Order to form a more perfect Union, establish Justice, insure
domestic Tranquility, provide for the common defence, promote the general Welfare, and secure the Blessings
of Liberty to ourselves and our Posterity, do ordain and establish this Constitution for the United States
of America.

The Preamble can be broken down into many important phrases. All of these phrases are very important for understanding the purpose of the United States Constitution.

We the people: This phrase means all the citizens of the United States of America. Even though the Constitution was written by some of the most well-educated men of the new country, the rights given under the document were given to all American citizens.

In order to form a more perfect union: The previous government was based on the Articles of Confederation, which were very limited. When the Framers wrote this, they felt that they were making new government that would be a better way to govern the country. (Kid.laws.com, 2015)

Establish justice: The reasons why there was Revolution against England were still important to the American citizens, so they wanted to make sure that they would have justice under the Constitution.

Insure domestic tranquility: One of the main reasons why the Constitutional Convention was held was because of Shays' Rebellion. This was an uprising of farmers in Massachusetts against the state for having to repay war debts. Citizens were worried with the keeping peace within the country's borders.

Provide for the common defense: There was still a change of being attacked by other countries. No individual state had the power to defend itself against attacks. Because of this, the Framers knew that it was important for the states to defend the nation together.

Promote the general welfare: This phrase meant that the well-being of the citizens would be taken care of as well as possible by the Federal government.

Secure the blessings of liberty to ourselves and our posterity: The point of this phrase in the Preamble, and the constitution as a whole was to help protect the country's hard-earned rights for liberty, unjust laws, and freedom from a tyrannical government.

Ordain and establish this Constitution for the United States of America: This last phrase of the Preamble is a powerful statement saying that the people made this document, and the people give the country its power.

(Kid.laws.com, 2015)

Even though the Preamble part for 'promoting the general Welfare' was intended for 'all citizens', over the years the phrase has been interpreted to expand government without regard to 'the general welfare' of all citizens.

Judge Andrew Napolitano's description of the 'General Welfare Clause':
"The other General Welfare Clause is in the first of the authorities given to the Congress and it's not a grant, it's a restriction. By which I mean it doesn't say Congress can legislate for the general welfare, it means that everything Congress must do has to enhance the general welfare of the United States of America.

It can't grant things to individuals, it can only legislate for the government."

In view of Judge Napolitano's and James Madison's interpretation of the General Welfare Clause the following analysis of the federal budget for 2015 will reflect the agency budgets that truly provide for the welfare of all citizens and not just a smaller group of individuals.

Constitutional Budget		2015 Budget
Defense (Common Defense)		644,077,000,000
Executive Branch (President)		549,000,000
Legislative Branch (Congress)		4,980,000,000
Judicial Branch (Establish Justice)		7,337,000,000
Treasury (Money System and Debt)		833,564,000,000
Commerce (General Welfare)		10,633,000,000
State and International Trade (General Welfare)		29,561,000,000
Subtotal	37%	1,530,701,000,000
Remaining Budget	63%	2,659,070,000,000
Total Budget FY 2015	100%	4,189,771,000,000

A budget based on the Constitution, as described by James Madison, is just 37% of the current budget for FY2015. The following table discloses those agency budgets that would be considered 'not promoting the general welfare' of all citizens or could best be administered by the individual state governments.

"Not Promoting the General Welfare?"	FY2015 Budget
Dept. of Health and Human Services	1,117,768,000,000
Dept. of Housing and Urban Development	41,710,000,000
Dept. of Homeland Security	45,837,000,000
Dept. of Agriculture	128,853,000,000
Dept. of Education	75,742,000,000
Dept. of Energy	29,976,000,000
Dept. of Labor	72,039,000,000
Dept. of the Interior	11,914,000,000

Dept. of Veterans Affairs	150,330,000,000
District of Columbia	899,000,000
Environmental Protection Agency	7,628,000,000
General Services Administration	747,000,000
Numerous Bureaus, Boards and Commissions	975,627,000,000
Total of Remaining Budget	2,659,070,000,000

Comparative Budget based on the U.S. Constitution of 1787

Constitutional Budget	FY2015	FY2014
Defense (Common Defense)	644,077,000,000	637,550,000,000
Executive Branch (President)	549,000,000	549,000,000
Legislative Branch (Congress)	4,980,000,000	5,025,000,000
Judicial Branch (Establish Justice)	7,337,000,000	7,275,000,000
Treasury (Money System and Debt)	833,564,000,000	725,673,000,000
Commerce (General Welfare)	10,633,000,000	10,672,000,000
State and International Trade (General Welfare)	29,561,000,000	30,649,000,000
Total Budget based on the Constitution	1,530,701,000,000	1,417,393,000,000
Remaining Budget	2,659,070,000,000	2,559,748,000,000
Total Budget	4,189,771,000,000	3,977,141,000,000

The following table illustrates the amount of tax receipts that would be left assuming the budget is based on the Constitution and the excess tax receipts (3,215,034,000,000 – 1,530,701,000,000 = 1,684,333,000,000) would be distributed to the states based on population in accordance with the 'general welfare' provision in the Preamble to the Constitution.

Amount to Distribute to the States	FY2015	FY2014
Gross Receipts	3,215,034,000,000	3,034,000,000,000
Less: Budget based on the Constitution	1,530,701,000,000	1,417,393,000,000
Excess Receipts distributed to the States	1,684,333,000,000	1,616,607,000,000

This calculation shows the amount necessary to cut the budgets for FY2015 and FY2014 to achieve a balanced budget at the federal level.

	FY2015	FY2014
Total Expenditure Budget	4,189,771,000,000	3,977,141,000,000
Less: Expenditures to the Constitution	1,530,701,000,000	1,417,393,000,000
Net Expenditures to cut in order to		
balance the budget at the federal level	2,659,070,000,000	2,559,778,000,000
	FY2015	FY2014
Gross Receipts for the Constitutional Budget	1,530,701,000,000	1,417,393,000,000
Expenditures for the Constitutional Budget	1,530,701,000,000	1,417,393,000,000
Balanced Constitutional Budget	0	0

This table identifies certain programs within each department or agency that appear to be unnecessary at the federal level and could possibly be better funded at the state level or eliminated all-together.

FY2015 Budget	Proposed Cuts	Remaining Budget
Health and Human Services	392,130,000,000	725,638,000,000
Housing and Urban Development	41,710,000,000	0
Homeland Security	19,663,000,000	26,174,000,000
Agriculture	105,498,000,000	23,357,000,000
Education	75,742,000,000	0
Energy	29,976,000,000	0
Labor	5,836,000,000	66,203,000,000

State	15,087,000,000	14,474,000,000
Interior	10,715,000,000	1,199,000,000
Veteran's Affairs	0	150,330,000,000
District of Columbia	0	899,000,000
Environmental Protection Agency	7,628,000,000	0
Social Security Administration	0	957,547,000,000
NASA	0	18,040,000,000
Other Personnel Management	0	91,066,000,000
Small Business Administration	874,000,000	0
Federal Drug Control Program	332,000,000	0
International Assistance Programs	25,317,000,000	0
Other Defense Civil Programs	0	60,645,000,000
Corps of Engineers	5,059,000,000	0
Administrative Conference of the U.S.	3,000,000	0
Advisory Council on Historical Preservation	6,000,000	0
Appalachian Regional Commission	73,000,000	0
Access Board	7,000,000	0
Barry Goldwater Scholarship	4,000,000	0
Central Intelligence Agency	0	514,000,000
Commission of Fine Arts	2,000,000	0
Commission on Civil Rights	9,000,000	0
Committee for Purchase from Disabled Persons	6,000,000	0
Commodity Futures Trading Commission	229,000,000	0
Consumer Product Safety Commission	112,000,000	0
Sub-Total	736,018,000,000	2,136,086,000,000

FY 2015 Budget	Proposed Cuts	Remaining Budget
Corporation for Public Broadcasting	457,000,000	0
United States Courts of Appeal for Veterans Claims	0	58,000,000
Defense Nuclear Facilities Safety Board	28,000,000	0
Equal Employment Opportunity Commission	369,000,000	0
Export-Import Bank of the United States	-307,000,000	0
Farm Credit System Insurance Corporation	0	-281,000,000
Federal Communications Commission	9,788,000,000	0
Federal Deposit Insurance Commission	0	-8,235,000,000
Federal Election Commission	0	65,000,000
Federal Financial Institutions Examination Council	0	2,000,000
Federal Labor Relations Authority	25,000,000	0
Federal Maritime Commission	24,000,000	0
Federal Mediation and Conciliation Service	46,000,000	0
Federal Mine Safety and Health Review Commission	21,000,000	0
Federal Retirement Thrift Investment Board	0	-140,000,000
Federal Retirement Thrift Investment Board	0	140,000,000
Federal Trade Commission	179,000,000	0
Harry S. Truman Scholarship Foundation	3,000,000	0
Institute of American Indian and Alaska Culture	9,000,000	0
United States Interagency Council on Homelessness	4,000,000	0
Sub-Total	10,646,000,000	-8,931,000,000

FY 2015 Budget	Proposed Cuts	Remaining Budget

International Trade Commission	94,000,000	0
James Madison Memorial Fellowship Foundation	2,000,000	0
Japan-United States Friendship Commission	3,000,000	0
Legal Services Corporation	435,000,000	0
Marine Mammal Commission	3,000,000	0
Merit Systems Protection Board	40,000,000	0
National Archives and Records Administration	0	388,000,000
National Capital Planning Commission	8,000,000	0
National Council on Disability	3,000,000	0
National Credit Union Administration	-1,432,000,000	0
National Endowment for the Arts and Humanities	289,000,000	0
National Labor Relations Board	278,000,000	0
National Mediation Board	14,000,000	0
National Science Foundation	7,626,000,000	0
National Transportation Safety Board	99,000,000	0
Neighborhood Reinvestment Corporation	207,000,000	0
Nuclear Regulatory Commission	121,000,000	0
Nuclear Waste Technical Review Board	3,000,000	0
Occupational Safety and Health Review Commission	13,000,000	0
Sub-Total	7,806,000,000	388,000,000

FY 2015 Budget	Proposed Cuts	Remaining Budget
Office of Government Ethics	14,000,000	0
Office of Navajo and Hopi Relocation	10,000,000	0
Office of Special Council	18,000,000	0

Railroad Retirement Board	0	7,052,000,000
Securities and Exchange Commission	0	-169,000,000
Smithsonian Institution	0	1,019,000,000
State Justice Institute	5,000,000	0
Tennessee Valley Authority	421,000,000	0
United States Holocaust Memorial Museum	51,000,000	0
United States Institute of Peace	49,000,000	0
Christopher Columbus Fellowship Foundation	1,000,000	0
Intelligence Community Management Fund	579,000,000	0
Institute of Museum and Library Services	233,000,000	0
United Mine Workers of America	26,000,000	0
Corporation for National and Community Service	1,243,000,000	0
United States Enrichment Corporation	-68,000,000	0
Morris K. Udall and Stewart L. Udall Foundation	6,000,000	0
Other Commissions and Boards	1,000,000	0
Chemical Safety and Hazard Investigation Board	11,000,000	0
Sub-Total	2,600,000,000	7,902,000,000

FY 2015 Budget	Proposed Cuts	Remaining Budget
Court Services for the District of Columbia	250,000,000	0
Presidio Trust	11,000,000	0
Denali Commission	16,000,000	0
Broadcasting Board of Governors	826,000,000	0
Delta Regional Authority	13,000,000	0
Vietnam Education Foundation		-5,000,000
Election Assistance Commission	11,000,000	0

Public Company Accounting Oversight Board	245,000,000	0
Standard Setting Body	7,000,000	0
Affordable Housing Program	216,000,000	0
Electric Reliability Organization	100,000,000	0
Office for Alaska Natural Gas Transportation Projects	4,000,000	0
Privacy and Civil Liberties Oversight Board	2,000,000	0
Federal Housing Finance Agency	244,000,000	0
Recovery Accountability and Transparency Board	31,000,000	0
Northern Border Regional Commission	2,000,000	0
National Railroad Passenger Corporation Office of Inspector General	21,000,000	0
Securities Investor Protection Corporation	-22,000,000	0
Patient - Centered Outcomes Research Trust Fund	492,000,000	0
Corporation for Travel Promotion	100,000,000	0
Bureau of Consumer Financial Protection	448,000,000	0
Civilian Property Realignment Board	-3,766,000,000	0
Allowances	-23,072,000,000	0
Undistributed Offsetting Receipts	-174,304,000,000	0
Sub-Total	-198,195,000,000	-5,000,000

Budget Summary	Proposed Cuts	Remaining Budget
Sub-Total, Page 1	736,018,000,000	2,136,086,000,000
Sub-Total, Page 2	10,646,000,000	-8,931,000,000
Sub-Total, Page 3	7,806,000,000	388,000,000
Sub-Total, Page 4	2,600,000,000	7,902,000,000

Sub-Total, Page 5	-198,195,000,000	-5,000,000
Total	558,875,000,000	2,135,440,000,000

This is a summary of the proposed cuts in programs within the many departments, agencies, and bureaus. The total of $558,575,000,000 only represents about 13% of the total budgeted expenditures.

The first two Articles of the Constitution identify the departments or agencies that are assumed to be necessary to enforce the new Constitution. Those departments and agencies identified with the Constitution are not reflected in this table.

This table displays bureaus and accounts contained within the budget for the Executive Office of the President. The display illustrates the length of time the program was funded in the annual budget. Some programs were dropped and picked up later in a 2nd budget period. The bureaus in bold identify those programs that have two budget periods that include FY2016.

Bureau Name	Account Name	1st Budget Period	2nd Budget Period
Armstrong Resolution	Armstrong Resolution Account	1994 to 2000	
Council of Economic Advisors	Salaries and Expenses	1962 to 2000	2008 to 2016
Council on Economic Quality	Council on Economic Quality	1971 to 2016	
Council on Economic Quality	Management Fund	1985 to 1996	2005 to 2006
Council on International Economic Quality	Salaries and Expenses	1972 to 1979	
Council on Wage and Price Stability	Salaries and Expenses	1975 to 1989	
Executive Office of the President	All Other Proprietary Receipts	2003 to 2010	
Executive Office of the President	Undistributed Payments	2004 to 2008	
Executive Residence at the White House	Operating Expenses	1962 to 2000	2008 to 2016
Executive Residence at the White House	Repair and Restoration	1997 to 1998	2008 to 2016
Expenses of Management Improvement	Expenses of Management Improvement	1962 to 1984	1989 to 1994
National Critical Materials Council	Salaries and Expenses	1986 to 1994	

Bureau Name	Account Name	1st Budget Period	2nd Budget Period
National Security Council and Homeland Security Council	Salaries and Expenses	1962 to 2000	2008 to 2016
National Space Council	Salaries and Expenses	1990 to 1994	
Office of Administration	Salaries and Expenses	1978 to 2000	2008 to 2016
Office of Drug Abuse Policy	Office of Drug Abuse Policy	1962 to 1974	1977 to 1978
Office of Management and Budget	Office of Management and Budget	1962 to 2016	
Office of National Drug Control Policy	Counterdrug Technology Assessment Center	1999 to 2000	
Office of National Drug Control Policy	Gifts and Donations	1988 to 1993	
Office of National Drug Control Policy	Gifts and Donations	1992	
Office of National Drug Control Policy	Office of National Drug Control Policy	1989 to 2016	
Office of National Service	Office of National Service	1994	
Office of Policy Development	Salaries and Expenses	1971 to 2000	
Office of Science and Technology Policy	Office of Science and Technology Policy	1963 to 2016	
Office of Telecommunication Policy	Salaries and Expenses	1966 to 1978	
Office of the United States Trade Representative	Office of the United States Trade Representative	1968 to 2016	
Presidential Transition	Administrative Support	2009 to 2010	
Special Action Office for	Special Action Office for Drug	1972 to 1987	

Bureau Name	Account Name	1st Budget Period	2nd Budget Period
Drug Abuse Prevention	Abuse Prevention		
Special Assistant to the President and Vice President	Donations for President Residence	1987 to 1994	
Special Assistant to the President and Vice President	Donations for Vice President Residence	1991 to 1993	
Special Assistant to the President and Vice President	Operating Expenses	1975 to 1994	
Special Assistant to the President and Vice President	Special Assistance	1971 to 2016	
The Points of Light Foundation	Salaries and Expenses	1983 to 1985	
The Points of Light Foundation	Salaries and Expenses	1991 to 1993	
The White House	Compensation of the President	1962 to 1994	
The White House	Compensation of the President and White House Office Staff	1962 to 2000	
The White House	The White House	2001 to 2016	
Unanticipated Needs	Emergency Response Fund	2002	
Unanticipated Needs	Information Technology Systems	1999	
Unanticipated Needs	Integrated Uses of Technology Information	2012 to 2016	
Unanticipated Needs	Iraq Relief and Reconstruction Fund	2003 to 2011	
Unanticipated Needs	Partnership Fund for Program Integrity Innovation	2010 to 2016	

Bureau Name	Account Name	1st Budget Period	2nd Budget Period
Unanticipated Needs	Spectrum Relocation Fund	2007	2012 to 2016
Unanticipated Needs	Unanticipated Needs	1962 to 1990	Various
Unanticipated Needs	Unanticipated Needs for Natural Disasters	1994	
White House Conference for a Drug-Free America	Salaries and Expenses	1987 to 1991	

CHAPTER 4

ASSIGNING CASH FLOW ACTIVITIES TO BUREAUS

Statement of Cash Flow

Operating Act ivities	Investing Activities	Financing Activities

The basis for the construction of a Statement of Cash Flows is to identify which financial statement components in the federal budget should be assigned to the three cash flow activities.

Operating Activities involve receipts and expenses that are an integral part of departmental operations…that is, operations represented by salaries, supplies, retirement contributions and does not include expenditures for capital assets or principal or interest payments on the federal debt.

Investing Activities reflect those activities that are expenditures for capital assets. Long-lived assets such as roads, highways, bridges, space program, and other assets that would benefit future years.

Financing Activities include transactions in the federal debt for principal and interest payments. Interest payments on the federal debt will be shown at the 'gross' amount and not offset by interest income as reported by the federal government.

The objective of the Statement of Cash Flow is to provide an understanding of cash flow that is generated and used by the three activities. Under normal operations, cash provided by operating activities would be a positive amount and used to purchase capital assets and pay on the federal debt without incurring additional debt.

Free Cash Flow is calculated in another chapter to illustrate the availability, or lack thereof, of cash available to pay on the federal debt. The calculation will illustrate the continued deficit spending and the continued reliance on borrowed money.

Cash Flow Activities

Operating Activities

Activities that involve the production, purchase of goods and supplies, and other expenses related to the operation of the agency and related bureaus.

Examples: Salaries and wages, office supplies and expense. (does not include expenditures for capital assets)

Investing Activities

Transactions that involve purchasing and construction of long-term assets.

Examples: Federal and State highways, bridges, housing, construction of government buildings and space vehicles.

Financing Activities

Transactions with creditors that involve obtaining cash from issuing debt and repaying amounts of principal and interest borrowed.

Examples: Sales of federal instruments primarily to foreign investors to cover federal budget deficits, and to pay for principal and interest payments as they become due. Some of the federal debt is held by government bureaus.

FY2014 Budget

Department	Operating Activities	Investing Activities	Financing Activities
Legislative Branch	5,025,000,000		
Executive Branch	549,000,000		
Department of Commerce	10,672,000,000		
Department of Energy	164,000,000	30,863,000,000	
Other Defense Civil Programs	58,986,000,000	174,000,000	
General Services Administration		860,000,000	
International Assistance Programs	23,728,000,000		
Department of Homeland Security	29,179,000,000	15,249,000,000	
Department of the Interior	7,343,000,000	4,784,000,000	
Department of Transportation	86,000,000	97,346,000,000	
Department of Justice	24,542,000,000	6,541,000,000	
Department of Education	69,878,000,000		
Department of the Treasury	150,621,000,000		575,052,000,000
Department of Labor	76,699,000,000		
Department of Defense	499,852,000,000	137,698,000,000	
Department of Health and Human Services	1,048,641,000,000		
Department of State	30,649,000,000		
Judicial Branch	7,275,000,000		
District of Columbia	898,000,000		
Department of Agriculture	135,507,000,000	1,168,000,000	
Department of Veterans Affairs	142,811,000,000		

Department of Housing and Urban Development	11,403,000,000	36,059,000,000	-3,853,000,000
Environmental Protection Agency	7,349,000,000		
Social Security Administration	908,222,000,000		
National Aeronautical and Space Admin		18,032,000,000	
Office of Personnel Management	87,255,000,000		
Small Business Administration	878,000,000		
Federal Drug Control Program	347,000,000		
Corp of Engineers	5,644,000,000		
Other (Separate List)	-287,035,000,000		
Total Activities	3,057,168,000,000	348,774,000,000	571,199,000,000
Total All Activities (Total Budget)	3,977,141,000,000		

Assignment of Activities
Legislative Branch

Bureaus	Budget FY2014	Operating	Investing	Financing
Senate	958,000,000	958,000,000		
House of Representatives	1,398,000,000	1,398,000,000		
Joint Items	18,000,000	18,000,000		
Office of Compliance	5,000,000	5,000,000		
Capitol Police	372,000,000	372,000,000		
Congressional Budget Office	46,000,000	46,000,000		
Architect of the Capitol	650,000,000	650,000,000		
Botanic Garden	11,000,000	11,000,000		
Library of Congress	633,000,000	633,000,000		
Government Printing Office	237,000,000	237,000,000		
Government Accountability Office	535,000,000	535,000,000		
United States Tax Court	58,000,000	58,000,000		
Legislative Branch Boards and Commissions	104,000,000	104,000,000		
Total Budget	5,025,000,000	5,025,000,000		

Assignment of Activities
Executive Branch

Bureaus	Budget FY2014	Operating	Investing	Financing
Executive Residence at the White House	14,000,000	14,000,000		
Special Assistance to the President and the Official Residence of the Vice President	5,000,000	5,000,000		
Council of Economic Advisers	4,000,000	4,000,000		
Council on Environmental Quality and Office of Environmental Quality	2,000,000	2,000,000		
National Security Council and Homeland Security Council	13,000,000	13,000,000		
Office of Administration	111,000,000	111,000,000		
Office of Management and Budget	89,000,000	89,000,000		
Office of National Drug Control Policy	22,000,000	22,000,000		
Office of Science and Technology Policy	6,000,000	6,000,000		
Office of the United States Trade Representative	49,000,000	49,000,000		
Unanticipated Needs	177,000,000	177,000,000		
Total Budget	549,000,000	549,000,000		

Assignment of Activities
Department of Commerce

Bureaus	Budget FY2014	Operating	Investing	Financing
Department of Commerce	20,000,000	20,000,000		
Departmental Management	132,000,000	132,000,000		
Economic Development Administration	421,000,000	421,000,000		
Bureau of the Census	1,259,000,000	1,259,000,000		
Economic and Statistical Analysis	108,000,000	108,000,000		
International Trade Administration	503,000,000	503,000,000		
Bureau of Industry and Security	106,000,000	106,000,000		
Minority Business Development Agency	30,000,000	30,000,000		
National Oceanic and Atmospheric Administration	5,363,000,000	5,363,000,000		
U.S. Patent and Trademark Office	-11,000,000	-11,000,000		
National Institute of Standards and Technology	1,283,000,000	1,283,000,000		
National Telecommunications and Information Administration	1,458,000,000	1,458,000,000		
Total Budget	10,672,000,000	10,672,000,000		

Assignment of Activities
Department of Energy

Bureaus	Budget FY2014	Operating	Investing	Financing
Department of Energy	-3,449,000,000		-3,449,000,000	
National Nuclear Security Administration	12,463,000,000		12,463,000,000	
Environmental and Other Defense Activities	6,301,000,000		6,301,000,000	
Energy Programs	14,392,000,000		14,392,000,000	
Power Marketing Administration	1,156,000,000		1,156,000,000	
Departmental Administration	164,000,000	164,000,000		
Total Budget	31,027,000,000	164,000,000	30,863,000,000	

Assignment of Activities Other Defense Civil Programs

Bureaus	Budget FY2014	Operating	Investing	Financing
Military Retirement	55,502,000,000	55,502,000,000		
Retiree Health Care	3,335,000,000	3,335,000,000		
Educational Benefits	126,000,000	126,000,000		
American Battle Monuments Commission	74,000,000		74,000,000	
Armed Forces Retirement Home	55,000,000		55,000,000	
Cemeterial Expenses	44,000,000		44,000,000	
Forest and Wildlife Conservation, Military Reservations	1,000,000		1,000,000	
Selective Service System	23,000,000	23,000,000		
Total Budget	59,160,000,000	58,986,000,000	174,000,000	

Assignment of Activities
Major Independent Bureaus

Bureaus	Budget FY2014	Operating	Investing	Financing
Corps of Engineers-- Civil Works	5,644,000,000		5,644,000,000	
Environmental Protection Agency	7,349,000,000	7,349,000,000		
National Aeronautics and Space Administration	18,032,000,000		18,032,000,000	
National Science Foundation	7,747,000,000	7,747,000,000		
Office of Personnel Management	87,255,000,000	87,255,000,000		
Small Business Administration	878,000,000	878,000,000		
Social Security Administration	908,222,000,000	908,222,000,000		
Total Budget	1,035,127,000,000	1,011,451,000,000	23,676,000,000	

Assignment of Activities
General Services Administration

Bureaus	Budget FY2014	Operating	Investing	Financing
General Services Administration	-77,000,000		-77,000,000	
Real Property Activities	595,000,000		595,000,000	
Supply and Technology Activities	13,000,000		13,000,000	
General Activities	329,000,000		329,000,000	
Total Budget	860,000,000		860,000,000	

Assignment of Activities International Assistance Programs

Bureaus	Budget FY2014	Operating	Investing	Financing
International Assistance Program	430,000,000	430,000,000		
Millennium Challenge Corporation	818,000,000	818,000,000		
International Security Assistance	13,718,000,000	13,718,000,000		
Multilateral Assistance	3,899,000,000	3,899,000,000		
Agency for International Development	6,039,000,000	6,039,000,000		
Overseas Private Investment Corporation	-237,000,000	-237,000,000		
Trade and Development Agency	68,000,000	68,000,000		
Peace Corps	465,000,000	465,000,000		
Inter-American Foundation	20,000,000	20,000,000		
African Development Foundation	24,000,000	24,000,000		
Military Sales Program	-1,521,000,000	-1,521,000,000		
Special Assistance Initiatives	5,000,000	5,000,000		
Total Budget	23,728,000,000	23,728,000,000		

Assignment of Activities
Department of Homeland Security

Bureaus	Budget FY2014	Operating	Investing	Financing
Department of Homeland Security	-5,781,000,000	-5,781,000,000		
Departmental Management and Operations	1,470,000,000	1,470,000,000		
Office of the Inspector General	153,000,000	153,000,000		
Citizenship and Immigration Services	2,933,000,000	2,933,000,000		
United States Secret Service	2,045,000,000	2,045,000,000		
Transportation Security Administration	4,100,000,000		4,100,000,000	
Federal Law Enforcement Training Center	297,000,000		297,000,000	
Immigration and Customs Enforcement	6,085,000,000	6,085,000,000		
Customs and Border Protection	12,691,000,000	12,691,000,000		
United States Coast Guard	10,852,000,000		10,852,000,000	
National Protection and Programs Directorate	1,520,000,000	1,520,000,000		
Federal Emergency Management Agency	6,504,000,000	6,504,000,000		
Science and Technology	1,211,000,000	1,211,000,000		
Domestic Nuclear Detection Office	348,000,000	348,000,000		
Total Budget	44,428,000,000	29,179,000,000	15,249,000,000	

Assignment of Activities
Department of the Interior

Bureaus	Budget FY2014	Operating	Investing	Financing
Department of the Interior	-6,574,000,000		-6,574,000,000	
Bureau of Land Management	1,491,000,000		1,491,000,000	
Bureau of Ocean Energy Management, Regulation and Enforcement	138,000,000		138,000,000	
Office of Surface Mining Reclamation and Enforcement	657,000,000		657,000,000	
Bureau of Reclamation	1,269,000,000		1,269,000,000	
Central Utah Project	33,000,000		33,000,000	
United States Geological Survey	1,092,000,000		1,092,000,000	
United States Fish and Wildlife Service	2,967,000,000		2,967,000,000	
National Park Service	3,193,000,000		3,193,000,000	
Bureau of Indian Affairs and Bureau of Indian Education	2,544,000,000	2,544,000,000		
Departmental Offices	2,706,000,000	2,706,000,000		
Insular Affairs	518,000,000		518,000,000	
Office of the Solicitor	65,000,000	65,000,000		
Office of Inspector General	47,000,000	47,000,000		
Office of the Special Trustee for American Indians	565,000,000	565,000,000		
National Indian Gaming Commission	19,000,000	19,000,000		
Department-Wide Programs	1,397,000,000	1,397,000,000		
Total Budget	12,127,000,000	7,343,000,000	4,784,000,000	

Assignment of Activities Department of Transportation

Bureaus	Budget FY2014	Operating	Investing	Financing
National Infrastructure Bank	2,121,000,000			2,121,000,000
Office of the Secretary	1,296,000,000	1,296,000,000		
Federal Aviation Administration	15,542,000,000		15,542,000,000	
Federal Highway Administration	53,421,000,000		53,421,000,000	
Federal Motor Carrier Safety Administration	746,000,000		746,000,000	
National Highway Traffic Safety Administration	1,085,000,000		1,085,000,000	
Federal Railroad Administration	6,563,000,000		6,563,000,000	
Federal Transit Administration	15,995,000,000		15,995,000,000	
Saint Lawrence Seaway Development Corporation	33,000,000		33,000,000	
Pipeline and Hazardous Materials Safety Administration	212,000,000		212,000,000	
Research and Innovative Technology Administration	18,000,000		18,000,000	
Office of Inspector General	86,000,000	86,000,000		
Surface Transportation Board	29,000,000		29,000,000	
Maritime Administration	518,000,000		518,000,000	
Total Budget	97,432,000,000	86,000,000	97,346,000,000	

Assignment of Activities
Department of Justice

Bureaus	Budget FY2014	Operating	Investing	Financing
General Administration	2,241,000,000	2,241,000,000		
United States Parole Commission	13,000,000	13,000,000		
Legal Activities and U.S. Marshals	6,113,000,000	6,113,000,000		
Radiation Exposure Compensation	104,000,000	104,000,000		
Interagency Law Enforcement	519,000,000	519,000,000		
National Security Division	84,000,000	84,000,000		
Federal Bureau of Investigation	7,788,000,000	7,788,000,000		
Drug Enforcement Administration	2,308,000,000	2,308,000,000		
Bureau of Alcohol, Tobacco, Firearms, and Explosives	1,106,000,000	1,106,000,000		
Federal Prison System	6,541,000,000		6,541,000,000	
Office of Justice Programs	5,037,000,000	5,037,000,000		
Total Budget	31,083,000,000	24,542,000,000	6,541,000,000	

Assignment of Activities
Department of Education

Bureaus	Budget FY2014	Operating	Investing	Financing
Office of Elementary and Secondary Education	19,446,000,000	19,446,000,000		
Office of Innovation and Improvement	4,405,000,000	4,405,000,000		
Office of Safe and Drug-Free Schools	1,610,000,000	1,610,000,000		
Office of English Language Acquisition	733,000,000	733,000,000		
Office of Special Education and Rehabilitative Services	16,549,000,000	16,549,000,000		
Office of Vocational and Adult Education	1,676,000,000	1,676,000,000		
Office of Postsecondary Education	2,883,000,000	2,883,000,000		
Office of Federal Student Aid	39,167,000,000	39,167,000,000		
Institute of Education Sciences	687,000,000	687,000,000		
Departmental Management	630,000,000	630,000,000		
Total Budget	69,878,000,000	69,878,000,000		

Assignment of Activities
Department of the Treasury

Bureaus	Budget FY2014	Operating	Investing	Financing
Financial Crimes Enforcement Network	109,000,000	109,000,000		
Departmental Offices	8,612,000,000	8,612,000,000		
Financial Management Service	24,831,000,000	24,831,000,000		
Federal Financing Bank	-464,000,000			-464,000,000
Alcohol and Tobacco Tax and Trade Bureau	518,000,000	518,000,000		
Bureau of the Public Debt	290,000,000			290,000,000
Internal Revenue Service	116,551,000,000	116,551,000,000		
Comptroller of the Currency	-44,000,000			-44,000,000
Interest on the Public Debt	671,245,000,000			671,245,000,000
Total Budget	725,673,000,000	150,621,000,000		575,052,000,000

Assignment of Activities
Department of Labor

Bureaus	Budget FY2014	Operating	Investing	Financing
Employment and Training Administration	76,090,000,000	76,090,000,000		
Employee Benefits Security Administration	190,000,000	190,000,000		
Pension Benefit Guaranty Corporation	-835,000,000	-835,000,000		
Office of Workers' Compensation Programs	2,392,000,000	2,392,000,000		
Wage and Hour Division	267,000,000	267,000,000		
Employment Standards Administration	8,000,000	8,000,000		
Occupational Safety and Health Administration	560,000,000	560,000,000		
Mine Safety and Health Administration	369,000,000	369,000,000		
Bureau of Labor Statistics	555,000,000	555,000,000		
Office of Federal Contract Compliance Programs	103,000,000	103,000,000		
Office of Labor Management Standards	39,000,000	39,000,000		
Departmental Management	559,000,000	559,000,000		
Total Budget	76,699,000,000	76,699,000,000		

Assignment of Activities
Department of Defense

Bureaus	Budget FY2014	Operating	Investing	Financing
Military Personnel	154,177,000,000	154,177,000,000		
Operation and Maintenance	223,154,000,000	223,154,000,000		
Procurement	120,519,000,000		120,519,000,000	
Research, Development, Test, and Evaluation	74,711,000,000	74,711,000,000		
Military Construction	15,225,000,000		15,225,000,000	
Family Housing	1,954,000,000		1,954,000,000	
Revolving and Management Funds	3,621,000,000	3,621,000,000		
Allowances	44,685,000,000	44,685,000,000		
Trust Funds	431,000,000	431,000,000		
Total Budget	637,550,000,000	499,852,000,000	137,698,000,000	

Assignment of Activities
Department of Health and Human Services

Bureaus	Budget FY2014	Operating	Investing	Financing
Food and Drug Administration	2,759,000,000	2,759,000,000		
Health Resources and Services Administration	9,459,000,000	9,459,000,000		
Indian Health Services	4,477,000,000	4,477,000,000		
Centers for Disease Control and Prevention	5,872,000,000	5,872,000,000		
National Institutes of Health	31,305,000,000	31,305,000,000		
Substance Abuse and Mental Health Services Administration	3,279,000,000	3,279,000,000		
Agency for Healthcare Research and Quality	132,000,000	132,000,000		
Centers for Medicare and Medicaid Services	1,343,554,000,000	1,343,554,000,000		
Administration for Children and Families	53,174,000,000	53,174,000,000		
Departmental Management	3,893,000,000	3,893,000,000		
Program Support Center	763,000,000	763,000,000		
Office of the Inspector General	51,000,000	51,000,000		
Total Budget	1,048,641,000,000	1,048,641,000,000		

Assignment of Activities
Department of State

Bureaus	Budget FY2014	Operating	Investing	Financing
Administration of Foreign Affairs	13,521,000,000	13,521,000,000		
Department of State	-158,000,000	-158,000,000		
International Commissions	120,000,000	120,000,000		
International Organizations and Conferences	3,742,000,000	3,742,000,000		
Other	13,424,000,000	13,424,000,000		
Total Budget	30,649,000,000	30,649,000,000		

Assignment of Activities
Judicial Branch

Bureaus	Budget FY2014	Operating	Investing	Financing
Administrative Office of the United States Courts	89,000,000	89,000,000		
Courts of Appeals, District Courts and Other	7,741,000,000	7,741,000,000		
Federal Judicial Center	29,000,000	29,000,000		
Judicial Branch	-646,000,000	-646,000,000		
Judicial Retirement Funds	182,000,000	182,000,000		
Supreme Court of the United States	96,000,000	96,000,000		
United States Court of Appeals for the Federal Circuit	34,000,000	34,000,000		
United States Court of International Trade	24,000,000	24,000,000		
United States Sentencing Commission	18,000,000	18,000,000		
Total Budget	7,275,000,000	7,275,000,000		

Assignment of Activities
District of Columbia

Bureaus	Budget FY2014	Operating	Investing	Financing
District of Columbia Courts	288,000,000	288,000,000		
District of Columbia General and Special Payments	610,000,000	610,000,000		
Total Budget	898,000,000	898,000,000		

Assignment of Activities
Department of Agriculture

Bureaus	Budget FY2014	Operating	Investing	Financing
Agricultural Marketing Service	2,561,000,000	2,561,000,000		
Animal and Plant Health Inspection Service	1,071,000,000	1,071,000,000		
Department of Agriculture	-891,000,000	-891,000,000		
Departmental Management	418,000,000	418,000,000		
Economic Research Service	83,000,000	83,000,000		
Farm Service Agency	11,048,000,000	11,048,000,000		
Food and Nutrition Service	98,432,000,000	98,432,000,000		
Food Safety and Inspection Service	980,000,000	980,000,000		
Foreign Agricultural Service	1,942,000,000	1,942,000,000		
Forest Service	5,481,000,000		5,481,000,000	
Grain Inspection, Packers and Stockyards Administration	42,000,000	42,000,000		
National Agricultural Statistics Service	160,000,000	160,000,000		
National Appeals Division	15,000,000	15,000,000		
National Institute of Food and Agriculture	1,373,000,000	1,373,000,000		
National Resources Conservation Service	4,322,000,000	4,322,000,000		
Office of Chief Economist	15,000,000	15,000,000		
Office of Communications	10,000,000	10,000,000		
Office of the General Council	44,000,000	44,000,000		
Office of the Inspector General	87,000,000	87,000,000		

Risk Management Agency	8,010,000,000	8,010,000,000		
Rural Business Cooperative Service	131,000,000	131,000,000		
Rural Development	235,000,000		235,000,000	
Rural Housing Service	933,000,000		933,000,000	
Rural Utilities Service	117,000,000		117,000,000	
Total Budget	136,675,000,000	129,909,000,000	6,766,000,000	

Assignment of Activities
Department of Veterans Affairs

Bureaus	Budget FY2014	Operating	Investing	Financing
Benefits Programs	81,420,000,000	81,420,000,000		
Department of Veterans Affairs	-3,563,000,000	-3,563,000,000		
Departmental Management	7,737,000,000	7,737,000,000		
Veterans Health Administration	57,217,000,000	57,217,000,000		
Total Budget	142,811,000,000	142,811,000,000		

Assignment of Activities
Department of Housing and Urban Development

Bureaus	Budget FY2014	Operating	Investing	Financing
Community Planning and Development	10,128,000,000	10,128,000,000		
Department of Housing and Urban Development	-901,000,000	-901,000,000		
Fair Housing and Equal Opportunity	74,000,000	74,000,000		
Government National Mortgage Association	-197,000,000			-197,000,000
Housing Programs	-3,656,000,000			-3,656,000,000
Management and Administration	1,769,000,000	1,769,000,000		
Office of Lead Hazard Control and Healthy Home	147,000,000	147,000,000		
Office of Sustainable Housing and Communities	122,000,000	122,000,000		
Policy Development and Research	64,000,000	64,000,000		
Public and Indian Housing Programs	36,059,000,000		36,059,000,000	
Total Budget	43,609,000,000	11,403,000,000	36,059,000,000	-3,853,000,000

Assignment of Activities
Environmental Protection Agency

Bureaus	Budget FY2014	Operating	Investing	Financing
Environmental Protection Agency	7,349,000,000	7,349,000,000		
Total Budget	7,349,000,000	7,349,000,000		

CHAPTER 5

STATEMENTS OF SPENDING FOR GOVERNMENT BUREAUS

The individual departmental budgets are prepared by the Office of Management and Budget (OMB) as a 'net' amount. That is, if a department has sources of income, those receipts are used to offset the appropriation necessary to fund operations, capital assets, and debt financing activities.

The following statements are prepared in accordance with GAAP standards for the Statement of Cash Flow. The sources of income are reported similar to gross revenue for a reporting entity and expenses are deducted from income to report the net amount needed to be funded by sales of federal debt instruments.

Further analysis will be necessary to determine if the projected sources of income are accurate, and if not, how will the shortage affect the appropriations for those departments?

The Statements of Spending will draw awareness to the massive detail within each department and raise questions concerning the necessity for many of the expenditures.

Statement of Spending
Department of Agriculture

		Budget
		FY 2015
Receipts for Operating Bureaus		
Payments to States and Possessions		-2,000,000
Administration of Rights-of-way and Other Land Uses		-4,000,000
Agriculture Credit Insurance, Negative Subsidies		-1,000,000
All Other General Fund Proprietary Receipts		-5,000,000
Charges, User Fees, and Natural Resource Utilization		-5,000,000
Commodity Credit Corporation Export Guarantee Financing, Negative Subsidies		-33,000,000
Deltas between the Annualized CR Amounts and the FY 2011 Budget Request		-13,000,000
Deposits of Fees, Inspection and Grading of Farm Products, AMS		-151,000,000
Deposits of Fees, Inspection and Grading of Farm Products		-10,000,000
Deposits of Miscellaneous Contributed Funds, APHIS		-17,000,000
Deposits of Miscellaneous Contributed Funds, Foreign Agricultural Service.		-1,000,000
Deposits of Miscellaneous Contributed Funds, Science and Education Administration		-18,000,000
Deposits, Acquisitions of Lands for National Forests, Special Acts		-1,000,000
Deposits, Brush Disposal		-13,000,000
Earnings on Investments, Native American Institutions Endowment Fund		-5,000,000
Facility Realignment and Enhancement Receipts		-1,000,000
Fees, Animal and Plant Health Inspection User Fee Account		-28,000,000
Fees, Food Safety Inspection User Fee Account		-12,000,000

Fees, Grain Inspection, Packers and Stockyards User Fee Account		-31,000,000
Forest Service Cooperative Fund		-56,000,000
Funds Retained, Stewardship Contracting Product Sales		-5,000,000
General Fund Payment, Funds for Strengthening Markets, Income, and Supply		-1,000,000
General Fund Proprietary Interest Receipts, not Otherwise Classified		-1,000,000
Gifts and Bequests, Departmental Administration		-1,000,000
Land Acquisition Proceeds for Exchanges		-29,000,000
Midewin National Tallgrass Prairie Rental Fees		-1,000,000
Miscellaneous Collections, Valles Caldera Fund		-1,000,000
Miscellaneous Contributed Funds		-1,000,000
Miscellaneous Special Funds, Forest Service		-3,000,000
National Forest Fund		-88,000,000
National Forests Fund, Payments to States		-3,000,000
National Forests Fund, Roads and Trails for States		-13,000,000
National Grasslands		-45,000,000
National Grasslands		-15,000,000
Negative Subsidies, Farm Storage Facility Loans		-7,000,000
Department of Agriculture (Cont.)		
NRCS Fees for Conservation Planning		-22,000,000
Payments from General Fund, Wool Research, Development, and Promotion Trust Fund		-2,000,000
Receipts, Cooperative Range Improvements		-3,000,000
Recreational Fee Demonstration Program, Forest Service		-67,000,000
Rents and Charges for Quarters, Forest Service		-10,000,000
Rural Community Facility, Negative Subsidies		-4,000,000
Rural Electrification and Telephone Loans, Negative Subsidies		-114,000,000

Rural Housing Insurance, Negative Subsidies		-7,000,000
Timber Roads, Purchaser Elections		-5,000,000
Timber Sales Pipeline Restoration Fund		-11,000,000
Timber Salvage Sales		-26,000,000
Agricultural Credit Insurance Fund Liquidating Account		-107,000,000
Commodity Credit Corporation Guaranteed Loans Liquidating Account		-7,000,000
State Mediation Grants		-2,000,000
Commodity Assistance Program		-1,000,000
Special Supplemental Nutrition Program for Women, Infants, and Children (WIC)		-1,000,000
Expenses, Public Law 480, Foreign Assistance Programs		-248,000,000
Forest Service Permanent Appropriations		-43,000,000
Farm Security and Rural Investment Programs		-118,000,000
Watershed Rehabilitation Program		-3,000,000
Rural Development Loan Fund Liquidating Account		-2,000,000
Rural Economic Development Grants		-149,000,000
Rural Housing Insurance Fund Liquidating Account		-514,000,000
Rural Development Insurance Fund Liquidating Account		-117,000,000
Rural Electrification and Telecommunications Liquidating Account		-786,000,000
Total Receipts for Operating Bureaus		-2,990,000,000

Statement of Spending
Department of Agriculture

	Budget	
	FY 2015	
Expenditures for Operating Bureaus		
Expenses and Refunds, Inspection and Grading of Farm Products	148,000,000	
Funds for Strengthening Markets, Income, and Supply (section 32)	51,000,000	
Funds for Strengthening Markets, Income, and Supply (section 32)	1,101,000,000	
Marketing Services	96,000,000	
Payments to States and Possessions	26,000,000	
Perishable Agricultural Commodities Act Fund	11,000,000	
Buildings and Facilities	21,000,000	
Miscellaneous Contributed Funds	18,000,000	
Salaries and Expenses	4,743,000,000	
Buildings and Facilities	5,000,000	
Miscellaneous Trust Funds	17,000,000	
Agriculture Buildings and Facilities and Rental Payments	247,000,000	
Departmental Administration	169,000,000	
Hazardous Materials Management	5,000,000	
Economic Research Service	83,000,000	
Agricultural Credit Insurance Fund Program Account	414,000,000	
Commodity Credit Corporation Export Loans Program Account	46,000,000	

Commodity Credit Corporation Fund	8,238,000,000	
State Mediation Grants	6,000,000	
Child Nutrition Programs	20,475,000,000	
Commodity Assistance Program	264,000,000	
Nutrition Programs Administration	164,000,000	
Special Supplemental Nutrition Program for Women, Infants, and Children (WIC)	7,140,000,000	
Supplemental Nutrition Assistance Program	63,796,000,000	
Expenses and Refunds, Inspection and Grading of Farm Products	10,000,000	
Food for Peace Title II Grants	1,800,000,000	
McGovern-Dole International Food for Education and Child Nutrition Program	223,000,000	
Public Law 480 Title I Direct Credit and Food for Progress Program Account	3,000,000	
Capital Improvement and Maintenance	339,000,000	
Forest and Rangeland Research	314,000,000	
Forest Service Payments to Communities	315,000,000	
Forest Service Permanent Appropriations	267,000,000	
Forest Service Trust Funds	112,000,000	
Land Acquisition	118,000,000	
National Forest System	1,645,000,000	
Range Betterment Fund	3,000,000	
State and Private Forestry	399,000,000	
Stewardship Contracting Product Sales	5,000,000	
Wildland Fire Management	2,042,000,000	
National Agricultural Statistics Service	160,000,000	
National Appeals Division	15,000,000	
Biomass Research and Development	10,000,000	

Extension Activities	456,000,000	
Integrated Activities	85,000,000	
Research and Education Activities	690,000,000	
Conservation Operations	867,000,000	
Farm Security and Rural Investment Programs	3,710,000,000	
Watershed and Flood Prevention Operations	23,000,000	
Watershed Rehabilitation Program	8,000,000	
Office of the Chief Economist	15,000,000	
Office of Communications	10,000,000	
Office of the General Counsel	44,000,000	
Office of the Inspector General	88,000,000	
Gifts and Bequests	1,000,000	
Healthy Foods, Healthy Neighborhoods Initiative	34,000,000	
Office of the Secretary	23,000,000	
Administrative and Operating Expenses	79,000,000	
Federal Crop Insurance Corporation Fund	7,985,000,000	
Bio refinery Assistance Program Account	15,000,000	
Rural Business Investment Program Account	1,000,000	
Rural Business Program Account	92,000,000	
Rural Cooperative Development Grants	36,000,000	
Rural Development Loan Fund Program Account	17,000,000	
Rural Energy for America Program	42,000,000	
Rural Microenterprise Investment Program Account	8,000,000	
Salaries and Expenses	225,000,000	
Multifamily Housing Revitalization Program Account	19,000,000	
Mutual and Self-help Housing Grants	7,000,000	

Rental Assistance Program	873,000,000	
Rural Community Facilities Program Account	42,000,000	
Rural Housing Assistance Grants	12,000,000	
Rural Housing Insurance Fund Program Account	458,000,000	
Distance Learning, Telemedicine, and Broadband Program	174,000,000	
Rural Electrification and Telecommunications Loans Program Account	39,000,000	
Rural Water and Waste Disposal Program Account	603,000,000	
Total Expenditures for Operating Bureaus		131,845,000,000
Net Operating Deficit to be funded by Federal Debt		(128,855,000,000)

Statement of Spending
Department of Homeland Security

		Budget
		FY 2015
Receipts for Operating Bureaus		
Breached Bond/detention Fund		-75,000,000
Fees, Aviation Security Capital Fund		-250,000,00
General Fund Proprietary Interest Receipts, not Otherwise Classified		-12,000,000
General Gift Fund		-1,000,000
H-1B and L Fraud Prevention and Detection Account		-105,000,000
H-1B Nonimmigrant Petitioner Account		-251,000.000
Immigrant Enforcement Account		-2,000.000
Immigration Examination Fee		-2,486,000.000
Immigration User Fee		-558,000.000
International Registered Traveler Program Fund		-3,000,000
Land Border Inspection Fee		-30,000,000
Marine Safety Fees		-18,000,000
Recoveries, Oil Spill Liability Trust Fund		-8,000,000
Student and Exchange Visitor Fee		-120,000,000
Tonnage Duty Increases		-24,000,000
US Customs User Fees Account, Conveyance/Passenger/Other		-505,000,000
US Customs User Fees Account, Merchandise Processing		-1,398,000,000
User Fees for Customs Services at Small Airports		-8,000,000
National Flood Insurance Fund		-252,000,000

Radiological Emergency Preparedness Program		-2,000,000
Federal Protective Service		-4,000,000
Total Receipts for Operating Bureaus		-6,112,000,000
Expenditures for Operating Bureaus		
Citizenship and Immigration Services	2,945,000,000	
Customs and Border Protection	13,094,000,000	
Department of Homeland Security	6,000,000	
Departmental Management and Operations	1,512,000,000	
Domestic Nuclear Detection Office	359,000,000	
Federal Emergency Management Agency	7,192,000,000	
Federal Law Enforcement	304,000,000	
Immigration and Customs Enforcement	6,260,000,000	
National Protection and Programs Directorate	1,569,000,000	
Office of the Inspector General	155,000,000	
Science and Technology	1,249,000,000	
Transportation Security Administration	4,052,000,000	
United States Coast Guard	11,148,000,000	
Secret Service	2,104,000,000	
Total Expenditures for Operating Bureaus		51,949,000,000
Net Operating Deficit to be funded by Federal Debt		(45,837,000,000)

Statement of Spending
Department of Health and Human Services

Receipts for Operating Bureaus	*FY2015*	
All Other General Fund Proprietary Receipts Including Budget Clearing Accounts	-56,000,000	
Basic Premium, Medicare Advantage, FSMI Trust Fund	-218,000,000	
Centers for Disease Control, Gifts and Donations	-6,000,000	
CLASS Independence Fund, Premiums	-11,600,000,000	
Contributions, Indian Health Facilities	-33,000,000	
Contributions, N.I.H., Conditional Gift Fund	-34,000,000	
Contributions, N.I.H., Unconditional Gift Fund	-7,000,000	
Cooperative Research and Development Agreements, Centers for Disease Control	-21,000,000	
Federal Contribution for Admin. Contribution for Admin. Costs, Prescription Drug Account, FSMI	-497,000,000	
Federal Contributions for Benefits, Prescription Drug Account, SMI	-71,054,000,000	
Federal Contributions, FSMI Fund	-222,403,000,000	
Federal Share of Child Support Collections	-763,000,000	
FHI Trust Fund, Basic Premium, Medicare Advantage	-193,000,000	
FHI Trust Fund, Medicare Refunds	-6,050,000,000	
FHI Trust Fund, Other Proprietary Interest from the Public	-2,000,000	
FHI Trust Fund, Payment from the General Fund for Health Care Fraud and Abuse Control Account	-138,000,000	
FHI Trust Fund, Payments from the General Fund (uninsured and Program Management)	-1,161,000,000	
FHI Trust Fund, Premiums Collected for Uninsured Individuals not Otherwise Eligible	-3,746,000,000	

Receipts for Operating Bureaus	***FY2015***	
FHI Trust Fund, Taxation on OASDI Benefits	-24,845,000,000	
FHI Trust Fund, Transfers from General Fund (civil Monetary Penalties)	-18,000,000	
FHI Trust Fund, Transfers from General Fund (criminal Fines)	-235,000,000	
General Fund Proprietary Interest Receipts, not Otherwise Classified	-90,000,000	
Interest, Child Enrollment Contingency Fund	-61,000,000	
Medicare Refunds, SMI	-4,550,000,000	
Miscellaneous Federal Payments, Federal Supplementary Medical Insurance Trust Fund	-1,000,000	
Other Proprietary Interest from the Public, FSMI Fund	-3,000,000	
Payments from States, Medicare Prescription Drug Account, FSMI	-10,106,000,000	
Premiums Collected for Medicare Prescription Drug Account, FSMI	-5,657,000,000	
Premiums Collected for the Aged, FSMI Fund	-66,330,000,000	
Premiums Collected for the Disabled, FSMI Fund	-12,244,000,000	
Rent and Charges for Quarters, Indian Health Service	-8,000,000	
Transfers from the Patient-Centered Outcomes Research Trust Fund	-44,000,000	
Health Education Assistance Loans Liquidating Account	-8,000,000	
Total Receipts for Operating Bureaus		-442,182,000,000
Total Expenditures for Operating Bureaus		
Administration for Children and Families	50,869,000,000	
Administration on Aging	2,460,000,000	
Centers for Disease Control and Prevention	5,785,000,000	
Centers for Medicare and Medicaid Services	1,445,111,000,000	
Department of Health and Human Services	31,000,000	

Receipts for Operating Bureaus	***FY2015***	
Departmental Management	3,461,000,000	
Food and Drug Administration	2,719,000,000	
Health Resources and Services Administration	9,917,000,000	
Indian Health Services	4,473,000,000	
National Institutes of Health	30,989,000,000	
Office of the Inspector General	52,000,000	
Program Support Center	817,000,000	
Substance Abuse and Mental Health Services Administration	3,266,000,000	
Total Expenditures for Operating Bureaus		1,559,950,000,000
Net Operating Deficit to be funded by Federal Debt		(1,117,768,000,000)

Statement of Spending
Department of Education

		Budget
		FY 2015
Receipts for Operating Bureaus		
All Other General Fund Proprietary Receipts		-47,000,000
Federal Direct Student Loan Program, Negative Subsidies		-12,594,000,000
Federal Perkins Loan, Negative Subsidies		-896,000,000
General Fund Proprietary Interest Receipts, not Otherwise Classified		-20,000,000
Repayment of Loans, Capital Contributions, Higher Education Activities		-28,000,000
Student Financial Assistance Debt Collection		-10,000,000
Undistributed Intragovernmental Payments		-4,000,000
English Learner Education		-48,000,000
Federal Family Education Loan Liquidating Account		-35,000,000
Health Education Assistance Loans Liquidating Account		-8,000,000
Perkins Loan Assets		-764,000,000
College Housing and Academic Facilities Loans Liquidating Account		-16,000,000
Supporting Student Success		-67,000,000
Total Receipts for Operating Bureaus		-14,537,000,000
Operating Bureaus		
Departmental Management	634,000,000	
Institute of Education Sciences	733,000,000	
Office of Elementary and Secondary Education	19,044,000,000	

Office of English Language Acquisition	770,000,000	
Office of Federal Student Aid	41,353,000,000	
Office of Innovation and Improvement	4,860,000,000	
Office of Postsecondary Education	2,865,000,000	
Office of Safe and Drug-Free Schools	1,786,000,000	
Office of Special Education and Rehabilitative Services	16,583,000,000	
Office of Vocational and Adult Education	1,651,000,000	
Total Operating Bureaus Expenditures		90,279,000,000
Net Operating Deficit to be funded by Federal Debt		(75,742,000,000)

Statement of Spending
Department of the Interior

		Budget
		FY2015
Receipts for Operating Bureaus		
Revolving Fund for Loans Liquidating Account		-1,000,000
Miscellaneous Permanent Payment Accounts		-6,000,000
Bureau of Reclamation Loan Liquidating Account		-1,000,000
Upper Colorado River Basin Fund		-5,000,000
Alaska Resupply Program		-3,000,000
All Other General Fund Proprietary Receipts Including Budget Clearing Accounts		-73,000,000
Central Valley Project Restoration Fund, Revenue		-56,000,000
Contributed Funds, Geological Survey		-1,000,000
Contributions and Deposits, BLM		-22,000,000
Deposits for Educational Expenses, Children of Employees, Yellowstone		-1,000,000
Deposits for Road Maintenance and Reconstruction		-2,000,000
Deposits, Contributed Funds, Fish and Wildlife Service		-4,000,000
Deposits, Operation and Maintenance, Indian Irrigation Systems		-30,000,000
Deposits, Reclamation Trust Funds		-3,000,000
Donations to National Park Service		-30,000,000
Earnings on Investment, Tribal Special Fund		-158,000,000
Federal Fund Payments, Tribal Trust Fund		-1,000,000
Forest Ecosystem Health and Recovery, Disposal of Salvage Timber		-2,000,000

		Budget
		FY2015
Receipts for Operating Bureaus		
Funds Reserved, Coos Bay Wagon Road Grant Lands		-1,000,000
Grazing Fees for Range Improvements, Taylor Grazing Act, As Amended		-8,000,000
Hardrock Mining Holding Fee		-16,000,000
Hardrock Revenues from Federal Lands		-6,000,000
Interest Earned, Environmental Improvement and Restoration Fund		-50,000,000
Interest on Investments in GSEs, Tribal Special Fund		-32,000,000
Land Sales, Southern Nevada Public Land Management		-2,000,000
Leases of Lands Acquired for Flood Control, Navigation, and Allied Purposes		-3,000,000
Miscellaneous Fees, Glacier Bay National Park Resource Protection		-3,000,000
Miscellaneous Sales of Assets, Tribal Trust Fund		-5,000,000
National Forests Fund, Payments to States		-8,000,000
National Wildlife Refuge Fund		-6,000,000
Natural Resources Damages from Legal Actions		-60,000,000
Park Concessions Franchise Fees		-85,000,000
Payment from the General Fund, Cooperative Endangered Species		-58,000,000
Payments to States and Counties from Land Sales		-2,000,000
Power Revenues, Indian Irrigation Projects		-73,000,000
Receipts from Grazing Fees, Federal Share		-8,000,000
Receipts from Mineral Leasing, Public Lands		-2,309,000,000
Receipts from Oil and Gas Leases, National Petroleum Reserve		-4,000,000
Reclamation Fund, Miscellaneous Interest		-13,000,000
Reclamation Fund, Other Proprietary Receipts from the Public		-151,000,000

		Budget
		FY2015
Receipts for Operating Bureaus		
Reclamation Fund, Royalties on Natural Resources		-1,880,000,000
Reclamation Fund, Sale of Public Domain		-13,000,000
Recreation Enhancement Fee Program		-197,000,000
Rent and Bonuses from Land Leases for Resource Exploration and Extraction		-48,000,000
Rental Payments, Park Buildings Lease and Maintenance Fund		-6,000,000
Rents and Charges for Quarters, Bureau of Indian Affairs		-35,000,000
Return of Principal from Private Sector Investments, Tribal Trust Fund		-545,000,000
Revenues, Colorado River Dam Fund, Boulder Canyon Project		-108,000,000
Royalties on Natural Resources, not Otherwise Classified		-473,000,000
Sale of Timber, Wildlife and Other Natural Land Products		-10,000,000
San Joaquin River Restoration Fund Receipts		-7,000,000
Service Charges, Deposits, and Forfeitures, BLM		-65,000,000
Surplus Land Sales, Federal Land Disposal Account		-29,000,000
Timber Sale Pipeline Restoration Fund		-1,000,000
Transfer from Lahonton Valley and Pyramid Lake Fish and Wildlife Fund		-1,000,000
Transportation Fees, Transportation System Fund		-16,000,000
Undistributed Intragovernmental Payments and Receivables		-39,000,000
User Fees for Filming and Photography on Public Lands		-1,000,000
Washington County, Utah Land Acquisition Account		-1,000,000
Assistance to Territories		-19,000,000
Land Acquisition and State Assistance		-9,000,000
Abandoned Mine Reclamation Fund		-3,000,000
Payments to States in Lieu of Coal Fee Receipts		-9,000,000

		Budget
		FY2015
Receipts for Operating Bureaus		
Cooperative Endangered Species Conservation Fund		-2,000,000
Mineral Leasing and Associated Payments		-41,000,000
Total Receipts for Operating Bureaus		-6,860,000,000
Expenditures for Operating Bureaus		
Bureau of Indian Affairs and Bureau of Indian Education	2,521,000,000	
Bureau of Land Management	1,541,000,000	
Bureau of Ocean Energy Management, Regulation and Enforcement	137,000,000	
Bureau of Reclamation	1,261,000,000	
Central Utah Project	31,000,000	
Departmental Offices	2,833,000,000	
Department-Wide Programs	1,279,000,000	
Insular Affairs	537,000,000	
National Indian Gaming Commission	19,000,000	
National Park Service	3,237,000,000	
Office of Inspector General	48,000,000	
Office of Surface Mining Reclamation and Enforcement	640,000,000	
Office of the Solicitor	65,000,000	
Office of the Special Trustee for American Indians	589,000,000	
United States Fish and Wildlife Service	2,940,000,000	
United States Geological Survey	1,096,000,000	
Total Expenditures for Operating Bureaus		18,774,000,000

		Budget
		<u>FY2015</u>
<u>Receipts for Operating Bureaus</u>		
Net Operating Deficit to be funded by Federal Debt		(11,914,000,000)

Statement of Spending
Department of Labor

		Budget
		FY 2015
Receipts for Operating Bureaus		
Deductions for offsetting receipts		-28,000,000
Unemployment compensation		-1,053,000,000
Other labor services		-44,000,000
Other interest		-2,156,000,000
Unemployment compensation		-348,000,000
Other labor services		-3,000,000
General retirement and disability insurance		-4,000,000
General retirement and disability insurance		-1,725,000,000
Unemployment compensation		-3,000,000
Total Receipts for Operating Bureaus		-5,364,000,000
Expenditures for Operating Bureaus		
Salaries and Expenses	2,572,000,000	
Deltas between the Annualized CR Amounts	4,000,000	
Information Technology Modernization	24,000,000	
Office of Disability Employment Policy	37,000,000	
Office of the Inspector General	75,000,000	
Veterans Employment and Training	48,000,000	
Working Capital Fund	10,000,000	
Federal Unemployment Benefits and Allowances	1,670,000,000	
Foreign Labor Certification Processing	44,000,000	

Office of Job Corps	1,667,000,000	
Program Administration	103,000,000	
State Unemployment Insurance	150,000,000	
States Paid Leave Fund	25,000,000	
TAA Community College	475,000,000	
Training and Employment Services	3,671,000,000	
Unemployment Trust Fund	64,489,000,000	
Administrative Expenses	142,000,000	
Black Lung Disability Trust Fund	667,000,000	
Energy Employees Occupational Illness	880,000,000	
Panama Canal Commission Compensation Fund	5,000,000	
Special Benefits for Disabled Coal Miners	496,000,000	
Special Workers' Compensation Expenses	149,000,000	
Total Expenditures for Operating Bureaus		77,403,000,000
Net Operating Deficit to be funded by Federal Debt		(72,039,000,000)

Statement of Spending
Department of the Treasury

	Budget	
Receipts for Operating Bureaus	<u>FY2015</u>	
Interest Received from Credit Financing Accounts	-71,167,000,000	
Proceeds, GSE Equity Related Transactions	-14,365,000,000	
Interest on Loans to Federal Financing Bank	-5,153,000,000	
Interest on Loans and Repayable Advances to the Federal Unemployment Account	-1,820,000,000	
Interest on Deposits in Tax and Loan Accounts	-1,165,000,000	
Charges for Administrative Expenses of Social Security Act, As Amended	-1,064,000,000	
Interest on Loans to National Flood Insurance Fund, DHS	-766,000,000	
All Other General Fund Proprietary Receipts	-510,000,000	
Interest on Loans to BPA	-469,000,000	
Interest on Loans or Advances to the Extended Unemployment Account	-440,000,000	
Exchange Stabilization Fund	-307,000,000	
Interest on Loans to Commodity Credit Corporation	-220,000,000	
Federal Financing Bank	-200,000,000	
Interest on Loans to Federal Deposit Insurance Corporation	-189,000,000	
Payment of Interest on Advances to the Railroad Retirement Board	-185,000,000	
New Installment Agreements, IRS Miscellaneous Retained Fees	-139,000,000	
Interest on Loans to the Helium Fund, Department of Interior	-130,000,000	
Interest on Loans to Temporary Corporate Credit Union Stabilization Fund	-129,000,000	

	Budget	
Receipts for Operating Bureaus	**FY2015**	
Interest Payments on Repayable Advances to Black Lung	-107,000,000	
Debt Collection	-78,000,000	
General User Fees, IRS Miscellaneous Retained Fees	-78,000,000	
Underpayment and Fraud Collection	-50,000,000	
Assessment Funds	-45,000,000	
Restructured Installment Agreements, IRS Miscellaneous Retained Fees	-36,000,000	
Interest on Quota in International Monetary Fund	-23,000,000	
Interest Payments from States, Cash Management Improvement	-23,000,000	
Interest on Advances to Colorado River Dam Fund, Boulder Canyon Project	-11,000,000	
Reimb.from Federal Agencies for Payments	-10,000,000	
Interest on Investment, Colorado River Projects	-9,000,000	
General Fund Proprietary Interest Receipts, not otherwise Classified	-5,000,000	
Gifts to the United States for Reduction of the Public Debt	-3,000,000	
Gifts to the United States, not Otherwise Classified	-3,000,000	
Interest on Loans to the Presidio	-3,000,000	
Interest on Loans for College Housing and Academic Facilities Loans	-2,000,000	
Earnings on Investments, Treasury Forfeiture Fund	-1,000,000	
Interest on Loans to the Secretary of Transportation	-1,000,000	
Treasury Franchise Fund	-1,000,000	
Total Receipts for Operating Bureaus		-98,907,000,000
Expenses for Operating Bureaus		
Department-wide Systems and Capital Investments Programs	1,000,000	

	Budget	
Receipts for Operating Bureaus	FY2015	
Payment of Government Losses in Shipment	1,000,000	
Check Forgery Insurance Fund	2,000,000	
Federal Interest Liabilities to States	2,000,000	
State Small Business Credit Initiative	6,000,000	
Interest on Uninvested Funds	8,000,000	
GSE Mortgage-Backed Securities Purchase Program Account	11,000,000	
Health Insurance Tax Credit Administration	18,000,000	
Payment to Issuer of New Clean Renewable Energy Bonds	28,000,000	
Payment to Issuer of Qualified Zone Academy Bonds	28,000,000	
Office of Inspector General	29,000,000	
Presidential Election Campaign Fund	37,000,000	
Payment in Lieu of Tax Credit for Growth Zones	43,000,000	
Special Inspector General for the Troubled Asset Relief Program	45,000,000	
Informant Payments	50,000,000	
Payment to Issuer of Qualified Energy Conservation Bonds	57,000,000	
Salaries and Expenses	68,000,000	
Small Business Lending Fund Program Account	77,000,000	
Salaries and Expenses	94,000,000	
Financial Research Fund	95,000,000	
Salaries and Expenses	109,000,000	
Reimbursements to Federal Reserve Banks	132,000,000	
Payment Where Health Coverage Tax Credit Exceeds Liability for Tax	147,000,000	
Treasury Inspector General for Tax Administration	152,000,000	
Administering the Public Debt	160,000,000	

	Budget	
Receipts for Operating Bureaus	**FY2015**	
Treasury Forfeiture Fund	195,000,000	
Business Systems Modernization	211,000,000	
Salaries and Expenses	212,000,000	
Community Development Financial Institutions Fund Program Account	218,000,000	
Treasury Forfeiture Fund	269,000,000	
Business Systems Modernization	300,000,000	
Salaries and Expenses	313,000,000	
Federal Reserve Bank Reimbursement Fund	333,000,000	
Small Business Health Insurance Tax Credit Exceeds Liability for Tax	357,000,000	
Terrorism Insurance Program	359,000,000	
Internal Revenue Collections for Puerto Rico	436,000,000	
Financial Agent Services	625,000,000	
Enforcement	715,000,000	
Claims, Judgments, and Relief Acts	848,000,000	
Payment to Issuer of Qualified School Construction Bonds	1,023,000,000	
Grants for Specified Energy Property in Lieu of Tax Credits	1,172,000,000	
Taxpayer Services	2,244,000,000	
Payment to the Resolution Funding Corporation	2,628,000,000	
Refunding Internal Revenue Collections, Interest	3,928,000,000	
Troubled Asset Relief Program, Home Affordable Modification	4,109,000,000	
Payment Where American Opportunity Credit Exceeds Liability	4,425,000,000	
Operations Support	5,068,000,000	
Enforcement	6,632,000,000	
Build America Bond Payments, Recovery Act	6,731,000,000	

	Budget	
Receipts for Operating Bureaus	**FY2015**	
Interest Paid to Expenditure Accounts - Shadow Account	9,052,000,000	
Interest Paid to Federal Fund Receipt Accounts - Shadow Account	13,972,000,000	
Interest Paid to Credit Financing Accounts	20,003,000,000	
Payment Where Child Tax Credit Exceeds Liability for Tax	25,586,000,000	
Refundable Premium Assistance Tax Credit	32,023,000,000	
Payment Where Earned Income Credit Exceeds Liability for Tax	45,893,000,000	
Interest Paid to Trust Fund Receipt Accounts - Shadow Account	197,457,000,000	
Interest on Treasury Debt Securities (gross)	544,004,000,000	
Total Expenses for Operating Bureaus		932,471,000,000
Net Operating Deficit to be funded by Federal Debt		(833,564,000,000)

CHAPTER 6

BUDGETS OF AGENCY BUREAUS

The agency budgets presented on following pages are shown as prepared by the Office of Management and Budget (OMB). Receipts that are specific to each agency are 'netted' against expenditures and therefore 'underreport' the actual expenditures for each agency.

The agency statements in Chapter 5 are 'grossed up' to reflect the estimated receipts that are supposedly used to fund expenditures. Further investigation is necessary to understand how expenditures are funded if the agency receipts do not meet budget estimates.

List of the Federal Bureaus in the Proposed Budget for FY2015

Agency	Bureaus	Programs
Legislative Branch	13	63
Judicial Branch	9	27
Department of Agriculture	25	175
Department of Commerce	12	48
Department of Defense	10	141
Department of Education	11	55
Department of Energy	6	53
Dept. of Health and Human Services	13	122
Dept. of Homeland Security	14	93
Dept. of Housing and Urban Development	10	81
Department of the Interior	17	188
Department of Justice	12	61
Department of Labor	12	57
Department of State	5	50
Department of Transportation	15	93
Department of the Treasury	10	94
Department of Veterans Affairs	4	47
Other Defense Civil Programs	8	19
International Assistance Programs	11	53
Executive Office of the President	12	15
General Services Administration	4	21
22- 25 Other Bureaus and Enterprises	103	221
Total	336	1977

The federal budget for FY 2015 contains 25 agencies with 336 bureaus, and 1,977 budgeted programs. Further analysis will focus on the individual agencies, their bureaus, and their budgeted programs.

Each analysis will be accompanied by an explanation of the purpose of the agency and its bureaus. Suspected abuses and questionable programs will be identified in each analysis.

FY 2014 Agency Budgets

Agency	Budget	Percent
Legislative Branch	5,025,000,000	.13%
Judicial Branch	7,275,000,000	.18%
Department of Agriculture	136,675,000,000	3.44%
Department of Commerce	10,672,000,000	.26%
Department of Defense	637,550,000,000	16.03%
Department of Education	69,878,000,000	1.76%
Department of Energy	31,027,000,000	.78%
Dept. of Health and Human Services	1,048,641,000,000	26.73%
Dept. of Homeland Security	44,428,000,000	1.12%
Dept. of Housing and Urban Development	43,609,000,000	1.10%
Department of the Interior	12,127,000,000	.30%
Department of Justice	31,083,000,000	.77%
Department of Labor	76,699,000,000	1.93%
Department of State	30,649,000,000	.77%
Department of Transportation	97,432,000,000	2.45%
Department of the Treasury	725,673,000,000	18.25%
Department of Veterans Affairs	142,811,000,000	3.59%
Other Defense Civil Programs	59,160,000,000	1.49%
International Assistance Programs	23,728,000,000	.60%
Executive Office of the President	549,000,000	.01%
General Services Administration	860,000,000	.02%
Major Independent Bureaus	1,035,127,000,000	26.03%
Other Independent Bureaus	-293,507,000,000	-7.38%
Government Sponsored Enterprises	0	0.00%
Financing Vehicles and the Board of Gov.	0	0.00%
Total Budget FY 2014	3,977,141,000,000	100.00%

Legislative Branch

Bureaus	FY2014 Budget
Senate	958,000,000
House of Representative	1,398,000,000
Joint Items	8,000,000
Office of Compliance	5,000,000
Capitol Police	372,000,000
Congressional Budget Office	46,000,000
Architect of the Capitol	50,000,000
Botanic Garden	11,000,000
Library of Congress	633,000,000
Government Printing Office	37,000,000
Government Accountability Office	535,000,000
United States Tax Court	58,000,000
Legislative Branch Boards and Commissions	104,000,000
Total Budget	5,025,000,000

Judicial Branch

Bureaus	FY2014 Budget
Supreme Court of the United States	82,000,000
United States Court of Appeals for the Federal Court	34,000,000
United States Court of International Trade	22,000,000
Courts of Appeals, District Courts, and other Judicial Services	7,462,000,000
Administrative Office of the United States Courts	85,000,000
Federal Judicial Center	27,000,000
Judicial Retirement Funds	214,000,000
United States Sentencing Commission	18,000,000
Total Expense Budget	7,944,000,000
Less: Receipts	-669,000,000
Total Budget	7,275,000,000

Executive Branch

Bureaus	FY2014 Budget
The White House	57,000,000
Executive Residence at the White House	14,000,000
Special Assistance to the President and the Official Residence of the Vice President	5,000,000
Council of Economic Advisers	4,000,000
Council on Environmental Quality and Office of Environmental Quality	2,000,000
National Security Council and Homeland Security Council	13,000,000
Office of Administration	111,000,000
Office of Management and Budget	89,000,000
Office of National Drug Control Policy	22,000,000
Office of Science and Technology Policy	6,000,000
Office of the United States Trade Representative	49,000,000
Unanticipated Needs	177,000,000
Total Budget	549,000,000

Department of Health and Human Services

Bureaus	FY2014 Budget
Food and Drug Administration	2,759,000,000
Health Resources and Services Administration	9,459,000,000
Indian Health Services	4,477,000,000
Centers for Disease Control and Prevention	5,872,000,000
National Institutes of Health	31,305,000,000
Substance Abuse and Mental Health Services Administration	3,279,000,000
Agency for Healthcare Research and Quality	132,000,000
Centers for Medicare and Medicaid Services	1,343,554,000,000
Administration for Children and Families	50,724,000,000
Administration on Aging	450,000,000
Departmental Management	3,893,000,000
Program Support Center	763,000,000
Office of the Inspector General	51,000,000
Total Expense Budget	1,458,718,000,000
Less: Receipts	-410,077,000,000
Total Budget	1,048,641,000,000

Department of Agriculture

Bureaus	FY2014 Budget
Office of the Secretary	56,000,000
Executive Operations	0
Departmental Management	418,000,000
Office of Communications	10,000,000
Office of the Inspector General	87,000,000
Office of Chief Economist	15,000,000
Office of the General Counsel	44,000,000
National Appeals Division	15,000,000
Economic Research Service	83,000,000
National Agricultural Statistics Service	160,000,000
Agricultural Research Service	1,129,000,000
National Institute of Food and Agriculture	1,373,000,000
Animal and Plant Health Inspection Service	1,071,000,000
Food Safety and Inspection Service	980,000,000
Grain Inspection, Packers and Stockyards Administration	42,000,000
Agricultural Marketing Service	1,427,000,000
Risk Management Agency	8,010,000,000
Farm Service Agency	11,048,000,000
Natural Resources Conservation Service	4,322,000,000
Rural Development	235,000,000
Rural Utilities Service	117,000,000
Rural Housing Service	933,000,000
Rural Business Cooperative Service	131,000,000
Foreign Agricultural Service	1,942,000,000
Food and Nutrition Service	98,432,000,000
Forest Service	5,481,000,000
Total Expense Budget	137,444,000,000
Less: Receipts	-891,000,000
Total Budget	136,670,000,000

Department of Defense

Bureaus	FY2014 Budget
Military Personnel	154,177,000,000
Operation and Maintenance	223,154,000,000
Procurement	120,519,000,000
Research, Development, Test, and Evaluation	74,711,000,000
Military Construction	15,225,000,000
Family Housing	1,954,000,000
Revolving and Management Funds	3,621,000,000
Allowances	44,685,000,000
Trust Funds	431,000,000
Total Expense Budget	638,477,000,000
Less: Receipts	-927,000,000
Total Budget	637,550,000,000

Department of Veterans Affairs

Bureaus	FY2014 Budget
Veterans Health Administration	57,217,000,000
Benefits Programs	81,420,000,000
Departmental Administration	7,737,000,000
Total Expense Budget	146,374,000,000
Less: Receipts	-3,563,000,000
Total Budget	142,811,000,000

Department of Labor

Bureaus	FY2014 Budget
Employment and Training Administration	76,090,000,000
Employee Benefits Security Administration	190,000,000
Pension Benefit Guaranty Corporation	-835,000,000
Office of Workers' Compensation Programs	2,392,000,000
Wage and Hour Division	267,000,000
Employment Standards Administration	8,000,000
Occupational Safety and Health Administration	560,000,000
Mine Safety and Health Administration	369,000,000
Bureau of Labor Statistics	555,000,000
Office of Federal Contract Compliance Programs	103,000,000
Office of Labor Management Standards	39,000,000
Departmental Management	559,000,000
Total Expense Budget	80,297,000,000
Less: Receipts	-3,598,000,000
Total Budget	76,699,000,000

Department of the Treasury

Bureaus	FY2014 Budget
Financial Crimes Enforcement Network	109,000,000
Departmental Offices	8,612,000,000
Financial Management Service	24,831,000,000
Alcohol and Tobacco Tax and Trade Bureau	518,000,000
Bureau of the Public Debt	290,000,000
Internal Revenue Service	116,551,000,000
Interest on the Public Debt	671,245,000,000
Total Expense Budget	822,156,000,000
Less: Receipts	-96,483,000,000
Total Budget	725,673,000,000

Department of Housing and Urban Development

Bureaus	FY2014 Budget
Public and Indian Housing Programs	36,059,000,000
Community Planning and Development	10,128,000,000
Policy Development and Research	64,000,000
Fair Housing and Equal Opportunity	74,000,000
Office of Lead Hazard Control and Healthy Homes	147,000,000
Office of Sustainable Housing and Communities	122,000,000
Management and Administration	1,769,000,000
Total Expense Budget	48,363,000,000
Less: Receipts	-4,754,000,000
Total Budget	43,609,000,000

Department of Education

Bureaus	FY2014 Budget
Office of Elementary and Secondary Education	19,446,000,000
Office of Innovation and Improvement	4,405,000,000
Office of Safe and Drug-Free Schools	1,610,000,000
Office of English Language Acquisition	733,000,000
Office of Special Education and Rehabilitative Services	16,549,000,000
Office of Vocational and Adult Education	1,676,000,000
Office of Postsecondary Education	2,883,000,000
Office of Federal Student Aid	39,167,000,000
Institute of Education Sciences	687,000,000
Departmental Management	630,000,000
Total Expense Budget	87,786,000,000
Less: Receipts	-17,908,000,000
Total Budget	69,878,000,000

Department of Justice

Bureaus	FY2014 Budget
General Administration	2,241,000,000
United States Parole Commission	13,000,000
Legal Activities and U.S. Marshals	6,113,000,000
Radiation Exposure Compensation	104,000,000
Interagency Law Enforcement	519,000,000
National Security Division	84,000,000
Federal Bureau of Investigation	7,788,000,000
Drug Enforcement Administration	2,308,000,000
Bureau of Alcohol, Tobacco, Firearms, and Explosives	1,106,000,000
Federal Prison System	6,541,000,000
Office of Justice Programs	5,037,000,000
Total Expense Budget	31,854,000,000
Less: Receipts	-771,000,000
Total Budget	31,083,000,000

Department of State

Bureaus	FY2014 Budget
Department of State	-158,000,000
Administration of Foreign Affairs	13,521,000,000
International Organizations and Conferences	3,862,000,000
Other	13,424,000,000
Total Expense Budget	30,807,000,000
Less: Receipts	-158,000,000
Total Budget	30,649,000,000

Department of Commerce

Bureaus	FY2014 Budget
Department of Commerce	20,000,000
Departmental Management	132,000,000
Economic Development Administration	421,000,000
Bureau of the Census	1,259,000,000
Economic and Statistical Analysis	108,000,000
International Trade Association	503,000,000
Bureau of Industry and Security	106,000,000
Minority Business Development Agency	30,000,000
National Oceanic and Atmospheric Administration	5,363,000,000
National Institute of Standards and Technology	1,283,000,000
National Telecommunications and Information Administration	1,458,000,000
Total Expense Budget	10,683,000,000
Less: Receipts	-11,000,000
Net Budget	10,672,000,000

Department of Transportation

Bureaus	FY2014 Budget
National Infrastructure Bank	2,121,000,000
Office of the Secretary	1,296,000,000
Federal Aviation Administration	15,542,000,000
Federal Highway Administration	53,421,000,000
Federal Motor Carrier Safety Administration	746,000,000
National Highway Traffic Safety Administration	1,085,000,000
Federal Railroad Administration	6,563,000,000
Federal Transit Administration	15,995,000,000
Saint Lawrence Seaway Development Corporation	33,000,000
Pipeline and Hazardous Materials Safety Administration	212,000,000
Research and Innovative Technology Administration	18,000,000
Office of the Inspector General	86,000,000
Surface Transportation Board	29,000,000
Maritime Administration	518,000,000
Total Expense Budget	97,665,000,000
Less: Receipts	-233,000,000
Total Budget	97,432,000,000

Department of Energy

Bureaus	FY2014 Budget
National Nuclear Security Administration	12,463,000,000
Environmental and Other Defense Activities	6,301,000,000
Energy Programs	14,392,000,000
Power Marketing Administration	1,156,000,000
Departmental Administration	164,000,000
Total Expense Budget	34,476,000,000
Less: Receipts	-3,449,000,000
Total Budget	31,027,000,000

Department of the Interior

Bureaus	FY2014 Budget
Bureau of Land Management	1,491,000,000
Bureau of Ocean Energy Management, Regulation and Enforcement	138,000,000
Office of Surface Mining Reclamation and Enforcement	657,000,000
Bureau of Reclamation	1,269,000,000
Central Utah Project	33,000,000
United States Geological Survey	1,092,000,000
United States Fish and Wildlife Service	2,967,000,000
National Park Service	3,193,000,000
Bureau of Indian Affairs and Bureau of Indian Education	2,544,000,000
Departmental Offices	2,706,000,000
Insular Affairs	518,000,000
Office of the Solicitor	65,000,000
Office of Inspector General	47,000,000
Office of the Special Trustee for American Indians	565,000,000
National Indian Gaming Commission	19,000,000
Department-Wide Programs	1,397,000,000
Total Expense Budget	18,701,000,000
Less: Receipts	-6,574,000,000
Total Budget	12,127,000,000

Department of Homeland Security

Bureaus	FY2014 Budget
Departmental Management and Operations	1,470,000,000
Office of the Inspector General	153,000,000
Citizenship and Immigration Services	2,933,000,000
United States Secret Service	2,045,000,000
Transportation Security Administration	4,100,000,000
Federal Law Enforcement Training Center	297,000,000
Immigration and Customs Enforcement	6,085,000,000
Customs and Border Protection	12,691,000,000
United States Coast Guard	10,852,000,000
National Protection and Programs Directorate	1,520,000,000
Federal Emergency Management Agency	6,504,000,000
Science and Technology	1,211,000,000
Domestic Nuclear Detection Office	348,000,000
Total Expense Budget	50,209,000,000
Less: Receipts	-5,781,000,000
Total Budget	44,428,000,000

Other Defense Civil Programs

Bureaus	FY2014 Budget
Military Retirement	55,502,000,000
Retiree Health Care	335,000,000
Educational Benefits	126,000,000
American Battle Monuments Commission	74,000,000
Armed Forces Retirement Home	55,000,000
Cemeterial Expenses	44,000,000
Forest and Wildlife Conservation, Military Reservations	1,000,000
Selective Service System	23,000,000
Total Budget	59,160,000,000

International Assistance Programs

Bureaus	FY2014 Budget
International Assistance Program	430,000,000
Millennium Challenge Corporation	818,000,000
International Security Assistance	13,718,000,000
Multilateral Assistance	3,899,000,000
Agency for International Development	6,039,000,000
Trade and Development Agency	68,000,000
Peace Corps	465,000,000
Inter-American Foundation	20,000,000
African Development Foundation	24,000,000
Special Assistance Initiatives	5,000,000
Total Expense Budget	25,486,000,000
Less: Receipts	-1,758,000,000
Total Budget	23,728,000,000

General Services Administration

Bureaus	FY2014 Budget
Real Property Activities	595,000,000
Supply and Technology Activities	13,000,000
General Activities	329,000,000
Total Expense Budget	937,000,000
Less: Receipts	-77,000,000
Total Budget	860,000,000

Major Independent Bureaus

Bureaus	FY2014 Budget
Corps of Engineers-Civil Works	5,644,000,000
Environmental Protection Agency	7,349,000,000
National Aeronautics and Space Administration	18,032,000,000
National Science Foundation	7,747,000,000
Office of Personnel Management	87,255,000,000
Small Business Administration	878,000,000
Social Security Administration	908,222,000,000
Total Budget	1,035,127,000,000

Other Independent Bureaus

Bureaus	FY2014 Budget
Architectural and Transportation Barriers Compliance Board	7,000,000
Administrative Conference of the United States	3,000,000
Advisory Council on Historic Preservation	5,000,000
Affordable Housing Program	216,000,000
Appalachian Regional Commission	74,000,000
Barry Goldwater Scholarship and Excellence in Education Foundation	4,000,000
Broadcasting Board of Governors	809,000,000
Bureau of Consumer Financial Protection	426,000,000
Central Intelligence Agency	514,000,000
Chemical Safety and Hazard Investigation Board	11,000,000
Christopher Columbus Fellowship Foundation	1,000,000
Civilian Property Realignment Board	78,000,000
Commission of Fine Arts	2,000,000
Commission on Civil Rights	9,000,000
Committee for Purchase from People who are Blind or Severely Disabled, Activities	6,000,000
Commodity Futures Trading Commission	226,000,000
Consumer Product Safety Commission	112,000,000
Corporation for National and Community Service	1,297,000,000
Corporation for Public Broadcasting	457,000,000
Corporation for Travel Promotion	100,000,000
Court Services and Offender Supervision Agency for the District of Columbia	248,000,000
Defense Nuclear Facilities Safety Board	29,000,000
Delta Regional Authority	12,000,000
Denali Commission	16,000,000
District of Columbia General and Special Payments	898,000,000
Election Assistance Commission	10,000,000
Electric Reliability Organization	100,000,000

Bureaus	FY2014 Budget
Equal Employment Opportunity Commission	366,000,000
Federal Communications Commission	10,787,000,000
Federal Drug Control Programs	347,000,000
Federal Election Commission	65,000,000
Federal Financial Institutions Examination Council Appraisal	2,000,000
Federal Housing Finance Agency	238,000,000
Federal Labor Relations Authority	25,000,000
Federal Maritime Commission	24,000,000
Federal Mediation and Conciliation Service	46,000,000
Federal Mine Safety and Health Review Commission	21,000,000
Federal Retirement Thrift Investment Board	0
Federal Trade Commission	179,000,000
Harry S. Truman Scholarship Foundation	3,000,000
Institute of American Indian and Alaska Native Culture and Arts Development	9,000,000
Intelligence Community Management Account	570,000,000
International Trade Commission	92,000,000
James Madison Memorial Fellowship Foundation	2,000,000
Japan-United States Friendship Commission	3,000,000
Legal Services Corporation	432,000,000
Marine Mammal Commission	3,000,000
Merit Systems Protection Board	40,000,000
Morris K. Udall and Stewart L. Udall Foundation	6,000,000
National Archives and Records Administration	389,000,000
National Capital Planning Commission	8,000,000
National Council on Disability	3,000,000
National Endowment for the Arts	147,000,000
National Endowment for the Humanities	144,000,000
Institute of Museum and Library Services	234,000,000
National Labor Relations Board	276,000,000
National Mediation Board	14,000,000
National Railroad Passenger Corporation Office of Inspector General	21,000,000
National Transportation Safety Board	98,000,000

Bureaus	FY2014 Budget
Neighborhood Reinvestment Corporation	207,000,000
Northern Border Regional Commission	2,000,000
Nuclear Regulatory Commission	122,000,000
Nuclear Waste Technical Review Board	3,000,000
Occupational Safety and Health Review Commission	13,000,000
Office of Government Ethics	14,000,000
Office of Navajo and Hopi Indian Relocation	10,000,000
Office of Special Counsel	18,000,000
Office of the Federal Coordinator for Alaska Natural Gas Transportation Projects	4,000,000
Other Commissions and Boards	1,000,000
Patient-Centered Outcomes Research Trust Fund	358,000,000
Presidio Trust	14,000,000
Privacy and Civil Liberties Oversight Board	2,000,000
Railroad Retirement Board	6,811,000,000
Recovery Act Accountability and Transparency Board	31,000,000
Public Company Accounting Oversight Board	234,000,000
Standard Setting Body	45,000,000
Securities Investor Protection Corporation	287,000,000
Smithsonian Institution	1,012,000,000
State Justice Institute	5,000,000
Tennessee Valley Authority	539,000,000
United Mine Workers of America Benefit Funds	29,000,000
United States Court of Appeals for Veterans Claims	57,000,000
United States Holocaust Memorial Museum	51,000,000
United States Institute of Peace	48,000,000
United States Interagency Council on Homelessness	4,000,000
Total Expense Budget	30,180,000,000
Less: Receipts	-323,717,000,000
Total Budget	-293,532,000,000

Agency Receipts FY2015 Comparison to Actual

Agency and Agency Number	2015 Budget	2015 Actual
1. Legislative Branch	-56,000,000	-38,000,000
2. Judicial Branch	-669,000,000	-669,000,000
5. Department of Agriculture	-3,195,000,000	-2,122,000,000
6. Department of Commerce	-114,000,000	-93,000,000
7. Department of Defense	-1,687,000,000	-1,688,000,000
9. Dept. of Health and Human Services	-410,262,000,000	-442,414,000,000
10. Department of the Interior	-6,665,000,000	-6,775,000,000
11. Department of Justice	-1,442,000,000	-801,000,000
12. Department of Labor	-4,444,000,000	-8,924,000,000
14. Department of State	-273,000,000	-269,000,000
15. Department of the Treasury	-97,218,000,000	-98,354,000,000
16. Social Security Administration	-38,782,000,000	-42,913,000,000
18. Department of Education	-18,902,000,000	-14,422,000,000
19. Department of Energy	-3,484,000,000	-3,590,000,000
20. Environmental Protection Agency	-1,282,000,000	-1,271,000,000
21. Department of Transportation	-790,000,000	-182,000,000
23. General Services Administration	-83,000,000	-82,000,000
24. Dept. of Homeland Security	-6,213,000,000	-5,995,000,000
25. Dept. of Housing and Urban Development	-6,672,000,000	-5,597,000,000
26. National Aeronautics and Space Administration	-16,000,000	-16,000,000
27. Office of Personnel Management	-44,801,000,000	-43,579,000,000
28. Small Business Administration	-1,000,000	0
29. Department of Veterans Affairs	-3,576,000,000	-3,573,000,000
100. Executive Office of the President	0	0
184. International Assistance Programs	-27,634,000,000	-25,907,000,000
200. Other Defense Civil Programs	-86,639,000,000	-90,449,000,000
202. Corps of Engineers – Civil Works	-518,000,000	-662,000,000

Agency and Agency Number	2015 Budget	2015 Actual
309. Appalachian Regional Commission	-8,000,000	-8,000,000
349. District of Columbia Courts	-617,000,000	-636,000,000
350. Equal Employment Opportunity Commission	-4,000,000	0
351. Export-Import Bank of the United States	-312,000,000	-258,000,000
355. Farm Credit System Insurance Corporation	-266,000,000	0
356. Federal Communications Commission	-163,000,000	-159,000,000
357. Federal Deposit Insurance Corporation	-1,393,000,000	-45,000,000
366. Federal Maritime Commission	-1,000,000	-1,000,000
369. Federal Retirement Thrift Investment Board	-139,000,000	-140,000,000
370. Federal Trade Commission	-10,000,000	-10,000,000
393. National Archives and Records Administration	-3,000,000	-4,000,000
415. National Credit Union Administration	-1,307,000,000	0
417. National Endowment for the Arts	-2,000,000	-1,000,000
422. National Science Foundation	-27,000,000	-27,000,000
429. National Regulatory Commission	-875,000,000	0
440. Postal Service	-531,000,000	-261,000,000
446. Railroad Retirement Board	-7,981,000,000	-8,098,000,000
449. Securities and Exchange Commission	-488,000,000	-518,000,000
476. United Mine Workers of America Benefit Funds	-211,000,000	-209,000,000
485. Corporation for National and Community Service	-226,000,000	-227,000,000
486. United States Enrichment Corporation Fund	-53,000,000	-68,000,000
487. Morris K. Udall and Stewart L. Udall Foundation	-10,000,000	-5,000,000
534. Office of the Federal Coordinator for Alaska Natural Gas Transportation Projects	-5,000,000	-5,000,000
537. Federal Housing Finance Agency	-48,000,000	-49,000,000
576. Securities Investor Protection Corporation	-38,000,000	-41,000,000
579. Patient-Centered Outcomes Research Trust Fund	-257,000,000	-527,000,000
900. Allowances	-23,207,000,000	-32,702,000,000
902. Undistributed Offsetting Receipts	-295,670,000,000	-311,237,000,000
Total Receipts and Trust Funds	-1,099,268,000,000	-353,974,000,000
Budget Over (Short) Actual	(745,294,000,000)	
Percentage Over (Short)	(68%)	

Note: The actual receipts for FY2015 are substantially below the budgeted amount for FY2015. Further analysis in other departments is necessary to establish the accuracy or inaccuracy of projected cash receipts. The effect on the budget results in more funds necessary to cover department expenses and unanticipated borrowings in the federal debt.

Future budgets should use the 'gross method' (Statements of Spending) to include cash receipts and cash disbursements that are compared to actual results for cash receipts and cash disbursements to properly evaluate the budgeting process.

CHAPTER 7

BUREAU OF ECONOMIC ANALYSIS (BEA) CATEGORIES

Mandatory and Discretionary Programs

FY2015 Budget

This section lists the budgets of each federal agency and the amount of discretionary and mandatory programs within each agency that are used by the Bureau of Economic Analysis (BEA) to produce economic statistical reports for the Department of Commerce.

The BEA analysis includes the budgets of each bureau contained within each federal agency and the discretionary and mandatory programs within each agency and bureau.

The BEA reports are considered to be dependable and often used to report on economic results or projections.

Budget Analysis
Bureau of Economic Analysis
Discretionary and Mandatory Classification

BEA is an agency of the Department of Commerce. Along with the Census Bureau, BEA is part of the Department's Economics and Statistics Administration.

BEA produces economic accounts statistics that enable government and business decision-makers, researchers, and the American public to follow and understand the performance of the Nation's economy. To do this, BEA collects source data, conducts research and analysis, develops and implements estimation methodologies, and disseminates statistics to the public. (BEA.gov, 2015)

BEA is one of the world's leading statistical bureaus. Although it is a relatively small agency, BEA produces some of the most closely watched economic statistics that influence the decisions made by government officials, business-people, households, and individuals. BEA's economic statistics, which provide a comprehensive, up-to-date picture of the U.S. economy, are key ingredients in critical decisions affecting monetary policy, tax and budget projections, and business investment plans. The cornerstone of BEA's statistics is the national income and product accounts (NIPAs), which feature the estimates of gross domestic product (GDP) and related measures. (BEA.gov, 2015)

The GDP was recognized by the Department of Commerce as its greatest achievement of the 20th century and has been ranked as one of the three most influential measures that affect U.S. financial markets. Since the NIPAs were first developed in the aftermath of the Great Depression, BEA has developed and extended its estimates to cover a wide range of economic activities. (BEA.gov, 2015)

Today, BEA prepares national, regional, industry, and international accounts that present essential information on such key issues as economic growth, regional economic development, inter-industry relationships, and the Nation's position in the world economy. (BEA.gov, 2015)

Discretionary spending refers to the portion of the budget that goes through the annual appropriations process each year. In other words, Congress directly sets the level of spending on discretionary programs. Congress can choose to increase or decrease spending on any of those programs in a given year.

https://www.nationalpriorities.org/budget-basics/federal-budget-101/spending/

Mandatory spending is largely made up of earned-benefit or entitlement programs, and the spending for those programs is determined by eligibility rules rather than the appropriations process. For example, Congress decides to create a program like the Supplemental Nutrition Assistance Program (SNAP), also known as food stamps. It then sets criteria for determining who is eligible to receive benefits from the program. The amount of money spent on SNAP each year is then determined by how many people are eligible and apply for benefits.

https://www.nationalpriorities.org/budget-basics/federal-budget-101/spending/

Bureau of Economic Analysis Category
Legislative Branch
FY2015 Budget

Bureau Name	Account Name	Amount	BEA Category
Architect of the Capitol	All Other General Fund Proprietary Receipts Including Budget Clearing Accounts	-2,000,000	Mandatory
Library of Congress	Contributions, Library of Congress Gift Fund	-11,000,000	Mandatory
Library of Congress	Contributions, Library of Congress Permanent Loan Account	-7,000,000	Mandatory
Library of Congress	Gift Shop, Decimal Classification, Photo Duplication, and Related Services	-1,000,000	Discretionary
Architect of the Capitol	Gifts and Donations	-1,000,000	Mandatory
Legislative Branch Boards and Commissions	Gifts and Donations, Open World Leadership Center Trust Fund	-1,000,000	Mandatory
Library of Congress	Income from Donated Securities, Library of Congress	-2,000,000	Net Interest
Architect of the Capitol	Judiciary Office Building Development and Operations Fund	-17,000,000	Discretionary
Legislative Branch Boards and Commissions	Payment from the General Fund, Open World Leadership Center Trust Fund	-13,000,000	Discretionary
Legislative Branch Boards and Commissions	Payments, John C. Stennis Center for Public Service Training and Development	-1,000,000	Mandatory
Total		-56,000,000	
Discretionary	-31,000,000		
Mandatory	-24,000,000		
Net Interest	-1,000,000		

Bureau of Economic Analysis Category
Judicial Branch
FY2015 Budget

Bureau Name	Account Name	Amount	BEA Category
Judicial Branch	Advances and Reimbursements, Judiciary Information Technology Fund	-426,000,000	Mandatory
Judicial Branch	Federal Payment to Claims Court Judges' Retirement Fund	-6,000,000	Mandatory
Judicial Branch	Federal Payment to Judicial Officers Retirement Fund	-106,000,000	Mandatory
Judicial Branch	Federal Payment to Judicial Survivors Annuities Fund	-13,000,000	Mandatory
Judicial Branch	Proceeds from Sale of Property, Judiciary Information Technology Fund	-118,000,000	Mandatory
Total		-669,000,000	

Bureau of Economic Analysis Category Department of Agriculture FY2015 Budget

Bureau Name	Account Name	Amount	BEA Category
Department of Agriculture	Administration of Rights-of-way and Other Land Uses	-4,000,000	Mandatory
Farm Service Agency	Agricultural Credit Insurance Fund Liquidating Account	-124,000,000	Mandatory
Department of Agriculture	Agriculture Credit Insurance, Negative Subsidies	-1,000,000	Discretionary
Department of Agriculture	All Other General Fund Proprietary Receipts Including Budget Clearing Accounts	-5,000,000	Mandatory
Department of Agriculture	Charges, User Fees, and Natural Resource Utilization, Land between the Lakes, Forest Service	-5,000,000	Mandatory
Food and Nutrition Service	Commodity Assistance Program	-2,000,000	Discretionary
Department of Agriculture	Commodity Credit Corporation Export Guarantee Financing, Negative Subsidies	-33,000,000	Mandatory
Farm Service Agency	Commodity Credit Corporation Guaranteed Loans Liquidating Account	-7,000,000	Mandatory
Department of Agriculture	Deltas between the Annualized CR Amounts and the FY 2011 Budget Request	-23,000,000	Discretionary
Department of Agriculture	Deposits of Fees, Inspection and Grading of Farm Products, AMS	-151,000,000	Mandatory
Department of Agriculture	Deposits of Fees, Inspection and Grading of Farm Products, Food Safety and Quality Service	-9,000,000	Mandatory
Department of Agriculture	Deposits of Miscellaneous Contributed Funds, APHIS	-17,000,000	Mandatory
Department of Agriculture	Deposits of Miscellaneous Contributed Funds, Foreign Agricultural Service.	-1,000,000	Mandatory
Department of Agriculture	Deposits of Miscellaneous Contributed Funds, Science and Education Administration	-18,000,000	Mandatory

Bureau Name	Account Name	Amount	BEA Category
Department of Agriculture	Deposits, Acquisitions of Lands for National Forests, Special Acts	-1,000,000	Mandatory
Department of Agriculture	Deposits, Brush Disposal	-13,000,000	Mandatory
Department of Agriculture	Earnings on Investments, Native American Institutions Endowment Fund	-5,000,000	Net Interest
Foreign Agricultural Service	Expenses, Public Law 480, Foreign Assistance Programs, Agriculture Liquidating Account	-261,000,000	Mandatory
Department of Agriculture	Facility Realignment and Enhancement Receipts, Acquisition of Lands to Complete Land Exchanges	-1,000,000	Mandatory
Natural Resources Conservation Service	Farm Security and Rural Investment Programs	-189,000,000	Discretionary
Department of Agriculture	Fees, Animal and Plant Health Inspection User Fee Account	-27,000,000	Mandatory
Department of Agriculture	Fees, Food Safety Inspection User Fee Account	-12,000,000	Mandatory

Bureau of Economic Analysis Category Department of Health and Human Services FY2015 Budget

Bureau Name	Account Name	Sub-function Title	BEA Category	Budget
Dept. of HHS	Federal Contributions, FSMI Fund	Medicare	Mandatory	-207,931,000,000
Dept. of HHS	Premiums Collected for the Aged, FSMI Fund	Medicare	Mandatory	-60,969,000,000
Dept. of HHS	Federal Contributions for Benefits, Prescription Drug Account, SMI	Medicare	Mandatory	-65,644,000,000
Dept. of HHS	FHI Trust Fund, Taxation on OASDI Benefits	Medicare	Mandatory	-21,555,000,000
Dept. of HHS	Payments from States, Medicare Prescription Drug Account, FSMI	Medicare	Mandatory	-9,559,000,000
Dept. of HHS	Premiums Collected for the Disabled, FSMI Fund	Medicare	Mandatory	-11,530,000,000
Dept. of HHS	FHI Trust Fund, Medicare Refunds	Medicare	Mandatory	-6,000,000,000
Dept. of HHS	Medicare Refunds, SMI	Medicare	Mandatory	-4,500,000,000
Dept. of HHS	FHI Trust Fund, Premiums Collected for Uninsured Individuals not Otherwise Eligible	Medicare	Mandatory	-3,653,000,000
Dept. of HHS	Premiums Collected for Medicare Prescription Drug Account, FSMI	Medicare	Mandatory	-4,939,000,000
Dept. of HHS	Federal Share of Child Support Collections	Medicare	Mandatory	-794,000,000
Dept. of HHS	FHI Trust Fund, Payments from the General Fund (uninsured and Program Management)	Medicare	Mandatory	-1,133,000,000
Dept. of HHS	Federal Contribution for Admin. Contribution for Admin. Costs, Prescription Drug Account, FSMI	Medicare	Mandatory	-489,000,000

Bureau of Economic Analysis Category Department of Health and Human Services FY2015 Budget

Dept. of HHS	FHI Trust Fund, Payment from the General Fund for Health Care Fraud and Abuse Control Account	Medicare	Mandatory	-135,000,000
Agency for Healthcare Research and Quality	Healthcare Research and Quality	Health research and training	Discretionary	132,000,000
Dept. of HHS	General Fund Proprietary Interest Receipts, not Otherwise Classified	Other interest	Net Interest	-90,000,000
Dept. of HHS	FHI Trust Fund, Basic Premium, Medicare Advantage	Medicare	Mandatory	-204,000,000
Dept. of HHS	Basic Premium, Medicare Advantage, FSMI Trust Fund	Medicare	Mandatory	-223,000,000
Dept. of HHS	All Other General Fund Proprietary Receipts Including Budget Clearing Accounts	Deductions for offsetting receipts	Mandatory	-56,000,000
Dept. of HHS	Contributions, Indian Health Facilities	Health care services	Mandatory	-33,000,000
Dept. of HHS	Cooperative Research and Development Agreements, NIH	Health research and training	Mandatory	-16,000,000
Dept. of HHS	FHI Trust Fund, Transfers from General Fund (civil Monetary Penalties)	Medicare	Mandatory	-17,000,000
Health Resources and Services Administration	Health Education Assistance Loans Liquidating Account	Health research and training	Mandatory	-8,000,000
Health Resources and Services Administration	Health Resources and Services	Health research and training	Mandatory	75,000,000
Dept. of HHS	Other Proprietary Interest	Other interest	Net Interest	-3,000,000

	from the Public, FSMI Fund			
Administration for Children and Families	Supporting Healthy Families and Adolescent Development	Social services	Mandatory	7,000,000
Dept. of HHS	Rent and Charges for Quarters, Indian Health Service	Health care services	Mandatory	-8,000,000

Bureau of Economic Analysis Category Department of Health and Human Services (Continued) FY2015 Budget

Dept. of HHS	FHI Trust Fund, Transfers from General Fund (criminal Fines)	Medicare	Mandatory	-230,000,000
Dept. of HHS	Cooperative Research and Development Agreements, FDA	Consumer and occupational health and safety	Mandatory	-3,000,000
Dept. of HHS	Cooperative Research and Development Agreements, Centers for Disease Control	Health research and training	Mandatory	-2,000,000
Dept. of HHS	Miscellaneous Federal Payments, Federal Supplementary Medical Insurance Trust Fund	Medicare	Mandatory	-1,000,000
Dept. of HHS	Contributions, N.I.H., Conditional Gift Fund	Health research and training	Mandatory	-34,000,000
Dept. of HHS	Centers for Disease Control, Gifts and Donations	Health research and training	Mandatory	-6,000,000
Dept. of HHS	Contributions, N.I.H., Unconditional Gift Fund	Health research and training	Mandatory	-7,000,000
Dept. of HHS	FHI Trust Fund, Other Proprietary Interest from the Public	Other interest	Net interest	-2,000,000
Dept. of HHS	Interest, Child Enrollment Contingency Fund	Other interest	Net interest	-60,000,000
Dept. of HHS	Deltas between the Annualized CR Amounts and the FY 2011 Budget Request	Social services	Discretionary	13,000,000
Administration on Aging	Aging Services Programs	Social services	Mandatory	10,000,000
Centers for Medicare and Medicaid Services	Grants to States for Premium Review	Health care services	Mandatory	49,000,000

Centers for Medicare and Medicaid Services	Temporary High Risk Health Insurance Pool Program	Health care services	Mandatory	442,000,000
Centers for Medicare and Medicaid Services	Temporary Reinsurance Program	Health care services	Mandatory	5,000,000

Bureau of Economic Analysis Category Department of Health and Human Services (Continued) FY2015 Budget

Centers for Medicare and Medicaid Services	American Health Benefit Exchange Program	Health care services	Mandatory	300,000,000
Departmental Management	Prevention and Public Health Fund	Health care services	Mandatory	1,150,000,000
Departmental Management	Pregnancy Assistance Fund	Health care services	Mandatory	25,000,000
Departmental Management	Health Insurance Reform Implementation Fund	Health care services	Mandatory	30,000,000
Centers for Medicare and Medicaid Services	Reduced Cost Sharing for Individuals Enrolling in Qualified Health Plans	Health care services	Mandatory	3,233,000,000
Departmental Management	World Trade Center Health Program Fund	Health care services	Mandatory	366,000,000
Health Resources and Services Administration	Maternal, Infant, and Early Childhood Home Visiting Programs	Health care services	Mandatory	389,000,000
Health Resources and Services Administration	Primary Health Care Access	Health care services	Mandatory	2,167,000,000
Centers for Medicare and Medicaid Services	Center for Medicare and Medicaid Innovation	Health care services	Mandatory	1,046,000,000
Centers for Disease Control and Prevention	Toxic Substances and Environmental Public Health, Agency for Toxic Substances	Health care services	Mandatory	3,000,000
Centers for Medicare and Medicaid	Child Enrollment Contingency Fund	Health care services	Mandatory	200,000,000

Services				
Administration on Aging	Class Independence Fund	Health care services	Mandatory	300,000,000
Department of Health and Human Services	CLASS Independence Fund, Premiums	Health care services	Mandatory	-10,300,000,000
Centers for Medicare and Medicaid Services	Reinsurance and Risk Adjustment Program Payments	Health care services	Mandatory	11,476,000,000
Departmental Management	General Departmental Management	Health care services	Mandatory	7,000,000
Department of Health and Human Services	Deltas between the Annualized CR Amounts and the FY 2011 Budget Request	Health research and training	Discretionary	39,000,000

Bureau of Economic Analysis Category
Department of Health and Human Services (Continued)
FY2015 Budget

Departmental Management	Transfers from the Patient-Centered Outcomes Research Trust Fund	Health research and training	Mandatory	-70,000,000
Administration for Children and Families	Low Income Home Energy Assistance	Other income security	Discretionary	1,000,000
Department of Health and Human Services	Deltas between the Annualized CR Amounts and the FY 2011 Budget Request	Other income security	Discretionary	-3,000,000
Food and Drug Administration	Revolving Fund for Certification and Other Services	Consumer and occupational health and safety	Mandatory	1,000,000
Administration for Children and Families	Payments to States for Foster Care and Adoption Assistance	Other income security	Mandatory	-2,000,000
Centers for Medicare and Medicaid Services	Health Care Fraud and Abuse Control Account	Medicare	Discretionary	640,000,000
Departmental Management	General Departmental Management	Health care services	Mandatory	-7,000,000
Centers for Disease Control and Prevention	Disease Control, Research, and Training	Atomic energy defense activities	Mandatory	61,000,000
Indian Health Services	Indian Health Facilities	Health care services	Mandatory	8,000,000
Centers for Disease Control and Prevention	Disease Control, Research, and Training	Health research and training	Mandatory	78,000,000
Food and Drug Administration	Salaries and Expenses	Consumer and occupational health and safety	Mandatory	4,000,000

Health Resources and Services Administration	Health Resources and Services	Health care services	Mandatory	1,000,000
Centers for Medicare and Medicaid Services	Program Management	Health care services	Mandatory	275,000,000
Administration for Children and Families	Payments to States for the Child Care and Development Block Grant	Other income security	Discretionary	9,000,000
Health Resources and Services Administration	Vaccine Injury Compensation Program Trust Fund	Health care services	Discretionary	19,000,000
Administration for Children and Families	Children and Families Services Programs	Social services	Mandatory	1,000,000
Administration for Children and Families	Supporting Healthy Families and Adolescent Development	Social services	Discretionary	-1,000,000
Administration on Aging	Aging Services Programs	Social services	Discretionary	-3,000,000

Bureau of Economic Analysis Category Department of Health and Human Services (Continued) FY2015 Budget

Departmental Management	Office for Civil Rights	Federal law enforcement activities	Discretionary	45,000,000
Program Support Center	HHS Accrual Contribution to the Uniformed Services Retiree Health Care Fund	Health care services	Discretionary	34,000,000
Administration for Children and Families	Children's Research and Technical Assistance	Other income security	Mandatory	48,000,000
National Institutes of Health	National Institutes of Health	Health research and training	Mandatory	131,000,000
Departmental Management	Office of the National Coordinator for Health Information Technology	Health care services	Discretionary	223,000,000
Administration for Children and Families	Supporting Healthy Families and Adolescent Development	Social services	Discretionary	63,000,000
Office of the Inspector General	Office of the Inspector General	Health care services	Discretionary	51,000,000
Centers for Disease Control and Prevention	Toxic Substances and Environmental Public Health, Agency for Toxic Substances	Health care services	Discretionary	74,000,000
Program Support Center	Miscellaneous Trust Funds	Health care services	Mandatory	82,000,000
Health Resources and Services Administration	Vaccine Injury Compensation Program Trust Fund	Health care services	Mandatory	249,000,000
Centers for Disease Control and Prevention	Disease Control, Research, and Training	Health research and training	Discretionary	40,000,000

Centers for Disease Control and Prevention	Disease Control, Research, and Training	Health research and training	Discretionary	-42,000,000
Administration for Children and Families	Refugee and Entrant Assistance	Other income security	Discretionary	114,000,000
Departmental Management	General Departmental Management	Health care services	Discretionary	167,000,000
Departmental Management	General Departmental Management	Health care services	Discretionary	187,000,000
Substance Abuse and Mental Health Services Administration	Substance Abuse and Mental Health Services	Health care services	Discretionary	431,000,000
Indian Health Services	Indian Health Facilities	Health care services	Discretionary	462,000,000

Bureau of Economic Analysis Category
Department of Health and Human Services (Continued)
FY2015 Budget

Administration for Children and Families	Contingency Fund	Other income security	Mandatory	612,000,000
Administration for Children and Families	Supporting Healthy Families and Adolescent Development	Social services	Mandatory	494,000,000
Administration for Children and Families	Children and Families Services Programs	Social services	Discretionary	383,000,000
Centers for Medicare and Medicaid Services	Medicare Prescription Drug Account, Federal Supplementary Insurance Trust Fund	Medicare	Discretionary	456,000,000
Program Support Center	Retirement Pay and Medical Benefits for Commissioned Officers	Health care services	Mandatory	647,000,000
Centers for Medicare and Medicaid Services	State Grants and Demonstrations	Health care services	Mandatory	503,000,000
Administration for Children and Families	Refugee and Entrant Assistance	Other income security	Discretionary	700,000,000
Departmental Management	Public Health and Social Services Emergency Fund	Health care services	Discretionary	113,000,000
Health Resources and Services Administration	Health Resources and Services	Health research and training	Discretionary	593,000,000
Centers for Medicare and Medicaid Services	Health Care Fraud and Abuse Control Account	Medicare	Mandatory	3,000,000
Food and Drug Administration	Salaries and Expenses	Consumer and occupational health and safety	Discretionary	2,754,000,000

Departmental Management	Public Health and Social Services Emergency Fund	Health care services	Discretionary	1,657,000,000
Administration on Aging	Aging Services Programs	Social services	Discretionary	2,143,000,000
Administration for Children and Families	Social Services Block Grant	Social services	Mandatory	1,785,000,000
Centers for Medicare and Medicaid Services	Federal Hospital Insurance Trust Fund	Medicare	Discretionary	2,571,000,000
Administration for Children and Families	Payments to States for the Child Care and Development Block Grant	Other income security	Discretionary	2,809,000,000
Centers for Disease Control and Prevention	Disease Control, Research, and Training	Health care services	Discretionary	1,878,000,000

Bureau of Economic Analysis Category Department of Health and Human Services (Continued) FY2015 Budget

Centers for Medicare and Medicaid Services	Federal Supplementary Medical Insurance Trust Fund	Medicare	Discretionary	3,164,000,000
Administration for Children and Families	Low Income Home Energy Assistance	Other income security	Discretionary	2,524,000,000
Indian Health Services	Indian Health Services	Health care services	Discretionary	4,007,000,000
Substance Abuse and Mental Health Services Administration	Substance Abuse and Mental Health Services	Health care services	Discretionary	2,848,000,000
Administration for Children and Families	Child Care Entitlement to States	Other income security	Mandatory	3,647,000,000
Health Resources and Services Administration	Health Resources and Services	Health care services	Discretionary	2,336,000,000
Health Resources and Services Administration	Health Resources and Services	Health care services	Discretionary	3,638,000,000
Centers for Disease Control and Prevention	Disease Control, Research, and Training	Health care services	Discretionary	3,780,000,000
Administration for Children and Families	Payments to States for Child Support Enforcement and Family Support Programs	Other income security	Mandatory	3,864,000,000
Administration for Children and Families	Payments to States for Foster Care and Adoption Assistance	Other income security	Mandatory	7,862,000,000

Centers for Medicare and Medicaid Services	Children's Health Insurance Fund	Health care services	Mandatory	11,336,000,000
Administration for Children and Families	Children and Families Services Programs	Social services	Discretionary	9,076,000,000
Administration for Children and Families	Temporary Assistance for Needy Families	Other income security	Mandatory	16,728,000,000
National Institutes of Health	National Institutes of Health	Health research and training	Discretionary	31,174,000,000
Centers for Medicare and Medicaid Services	Medicare Prescription Drug Account, Federal Supplementary Insurance Trust Fund	Medicare	Mandatory	80,137,000,000
Centers for Medicare and Medicaid Services	Federal Supplementary Medical Insurance Trust Fund	Medicare	Mandatory	281,418,000,000
Centers for Medicare and Medicaid Services	Payments to Health Care Trust Funds	Medicare	Mandatory	297,132,000,000
Centers for Medicare and Medicaid Services	Grants to States for Medicaid	Health care services	Mandatory	352,141,000,000
Centers for Medicare and Medicaid Services	Federal Hospital Insurance Trust Fund	Medicare	Mandatory	297,027,000,000
Total				1,048,641,000,000

Bureau of Economic Analysis Category
HHS Budget Summary
Administration for Children and Families
FY2015 Budget

Account Name	Sub-function Title	BEA Category	Budget
Temporary Assistance for Needy Families	Other income security	Mandatory	16,728,000,000
Children and Families Services Programs	Social services	Discretionary	9,076,000,000
Payments to States for Foster Care and Adoption Assistance	Other income security	Mandatory	7,862,000,000
Payments to States for Child Support Enforcement and Family Support Programs	Other income security	Mandatory	3,864,000,000
Child Care Entitlement to States	Other income security	Mandatory	3,647,000,000
Payments to States for the Child Care and Development Block Grant	Other income security	Discretionary	2,809,000,000
Low Income Home Energy Assistance	Other income security	Discretionary	2,524,000,000
Social Services Block Grant	Social services	Mandatory	1,785,000,000
Refugee and Entrant Assistance	Other income security	Discretionary	700,000,000
Contingency Fund	Other income security	Mandatory	612,000,000
Supporting Healthy Families and Adolescent Development	Social services	Mandatory	494,000,000
Children and Families Services Programs	Social services	Discretionary	383,000,000
Refugee and Entrant Assistance	Other income security	Discretionary	114,000,000
Supporting Healthy Families and Adolescent Development	Social services	Discretionary	63,000,000
Children's Research and Technical Assistance	Other income security	Mandatory	48,000,000
Payments to States for the Child Care and Development Block Grant	Other income security	Discretionary	9,000,000
Supporting Healthy Families and Adolescent Development	Social services	Mandatory	7,000,000

Low Income Home Energy Assistance	Other income security	Discretionary	1,000,000
Children and Families Services Programs	Social services	Mandatory	1,000,000
Supporting Healthy Families and Adolescent Development	Social services	Discretionary	-1,000,000
Payments to States for Foster Care and Adoption Assistance	Other income security	Mandatory	-2,000,000
Total – Administration for Children and Families			50,724,000,000

Bureau of Economic Analysis Category HHS Budget Summary Administration on Aging FY2015 Budget

Account Name	Sub-function Title	BEA Category	Budget
Aging Services Programs	Social services	Discretionary	2,143,000,000
Class Independence Fund	Health care services	Mandatory	300,000,000
Aging Services Programs	Social services	Mandatory	10,000,000
Aging Services Programs	Social services	Discretionary	-3,000,000
Total – Administration on Aging			2,450,000,000

Bureau of Economic Analysis Category
HHS Budget Summary
Agency for Healthcare Research and Quality
FY2015 Budget

Account Name	Sub-function Title	BEA Category	Budget
Healthcare research and quality	Health research and training	Mandatory	132,000,000
Total – Healthcare Research and Quality			132,000,000

Bureau of Economic Analysis Category
HHS Budget Summary
Centers for Disease Control and Prevention
FY2015 Budget

Account Name	Sub-function Title	BEA Category	Budget
Disease Control, Research, and Training	Health care services	Discretionary	3,780,000,000
Disease Control, Research, and Training	Health care services	Discretionary	1,878,000,000
Disease Control, Research, and Training	Health research and training	Mandatory	78,000,000
Toxic Substances and Environmental Public Health, Agency for Toxic Substances	Health care services	Discretionary	74,000,000
Disease Control, Research, and Training	Atomic energy defense activities	Mandatory	61,000,000
Disease Control, Research, and Training	Health research and training	Discretionary	40,000,000
Toxic Substances and Environmental Public Health, Agency for Toxic Substances	Health care services	Mandatory	3,000,000
Disease Control, Research, and Training	Health research and training	Discretionary	-42,000,000
Total – Centers for Disease Control and Prevention			5,872,000,000

Bureau of Economic Analysis Category HHS Budget Summary Centers for Medicare and Medicaid FY2015 Budget

Account Name	Sub-function Title	BEA Category	Budget
Grants to States for Medicaid	Health care services	Mandatory	352,141,000,000
Payments to Health Care Trust Funds	Medicare	Mandatory	297,132,000,000
Federal Hospital Insurance Trust Fund	Medicare	Mandatory	297,027,000,000
Federal Supplementary Medical Insurance Trust Fund	Medicare	Mandatory	281,418,000,000
Medicare Prescription Drug Account, Federal Supplementary Insurance Trust Fund	Medicare	Mandatory	80,137,000,000
Reinsurance and Risk Adjustment Program Payments	Health care services	Mandatory	11,476,000,000
Children's Health Insurance Fund	Health care services	Mandatory	11,336,000,000
Reduced Cost Sharing for Individuals Enrolling in Qualified Health Plans	Health care services	Mandatory	3,233,000,000
Federal Supplementary Medical Insurance Trust Fund	Medicare	Discretionary	3,164,000,000
Federal Hospital Insurance Trust Fund	Medicare	Discretionary	2,571,000,000
Center for Medicare and Medicaid Innovation	Health care services	Mandatory	1,046,000,000
Health Care Fraud and Abuse Control Account	Medicare	Discretionary	640,000,000
State Grants and Demonstrations	Health care services	Mandatory	503,000,000
Medicare Prescription Drug Account, Federal Supplementary Insurance Trust Fund	Medicare	Discretionary	456,000,000
Temporary High Risk Health Insurance Pool Program	Health care services	Mandatory	442,000,000
American Health Benefit Exchange Program	Health care services	Mandatory	300,000,000
Program Management	Health care services	Mandatory	275,000,000

Child Enrollment Contingency Fund	Health care services	Mandatory	200,000,000
Grants to States for Premium Review	Health care services	Mandatory	49,000,000
Temporary Reinsurance Program	Health care services	Mandatory	5,000,000
Health Care Fraud and Abuse Control Account	Medicare	Mandatory	3,000,000
Total – Centers for Medicare and Medicaid Services			1,343,554,000,000

Bureau of Economic Analysis Category HHS Budget Summary Department of Health and Human Services FY2015 Budget

Account Name	Sub-function Title	BEA Category	Budget
Deltas between the Annualized CR Amounts and the FY 2011 Budget Request	Health research and training	Discretionary	39,000,000
Deltas between the Annualized CR Amounts and the FY 2011 Budget Request	Social services	Discretionary	13,000,000
Miscellaneous Federal Payments, Federal Supplementary Medical Insurance Trust Fund	Medicare	Mandatory	-1,000,000
Cooperative Research and Development Agreements, Centers for Disease Control	Health research and training	Mandatory	-2,000,000
FHI Trust Fund, Other Proprietary Interest from the Public	Other interest	Net interest	-2,000,000
Cooperative Research and Development Agreements, FDA	Consumer and occupational health and safety	Mandatory	-3,000,000
Deltas between the Annualized CR Amounts and the FY 2011 Budget Request	Other income security	Discretionary	-3,000,000
Other Proprietary Interest from the Public, FSMI Fund	Other interest	Net interest	-3,000,000
Centers for Disease Control, Gifts and Donations	Health research and training	Mandatory	-6,000,000
Contributions, N.I.H., Unconditional Gift Fund	Health research and training	Mandatory	-7,000,000
Rent and Charges for Quarters, Indian Health Service	Health care services	Mandatory	-8,000,000
Cooperative Research and Development Agreements, NIH	Health research and training	Mandatory	-16,000,000
FHI Trust Fund, Transfers from General Fund (civil Monetary Penalties)	Medicare	Mandatory	-17,000,000
Contributions, Indian Health Facilities	Health care services	Mandatory	-33,000,000
Contributions, N.I.H., Conditional Gift Fund	Health research and training	Mandatory	-34,000,000

All Other General Fund Proprietary Receipts Including Budget Clearing Accounts	Deductions for offsetting receipts	Mandatory	-56,000,000
Interest, Child Enrollment Contingency Fund	Other interest	Net interest	-60,000,000

Bureau of Economic Analysis Category HHS Budget Summary Department of Health and Human Services FY2015 Budget

Account Name	Sub-function Title	BEA Category	Budget
General Fund Proprietary Interest Receipts, not Otherwise Classified	Other interest	Net interest	-90,000,000
FHI Trust Fund, Payment from the General Fund for Health Care Fraud and Abuse Control Account	Medicare	Mandatory	-135,000,000
FHI Trust Fund, Basic Premium, Medicare Advantage	Medicare	Mandatory	-204,000,000
Basic Premium, Medicare Advantage, FSMI Trust Fund	Medicare	Mandatory	-223,000,000
FHI Trust Fund, Transfers from General Fund (Criminal Fines)	Medicare	Mandatory	-230,000,000
Federal Contribution for Admin. Contribution for Admin. Costs, Prescription Drug Account, FSMI	Medicare	Mandatory	-489,000,000
Federal Share of Child Support Collections	Other income security	Mandatory	-794,000,000
FHI Trust Fund, Payments from the General Fund (uninsured and Program Management)	Medicare	Mandatory	-1,133,000,000
FHI Trust Fund, Premiums Collected for Uninsured Individuals not Otherwise Eligible	Medicare	Mandatory	-3,653,000,000
Medicare Refunds, SMI	Medicare	Mandatory	-4,500,000,000
Premiums Collected for Medicare Prescription Drug Account, FSMI	Medicare	Mandatory	-4,939,000,000
FHI Trust Fund, Medicare Refunds	Medicare	Mandatory	-6,000,000,000
Payments from States, Medicare Prescription Drug Account, FSMI	Medicare	Mandatory	-9,559,000,000
CLASS Independence Fund, Premiums	Health care services	Mandatory	-10,300,000,000

Premiums Collected for the Disabled, FSMI Fund	Medicare	Mandatory	-11,530,000,000
FHI Trust Fund, Taxation on OASDI Benefits	Medicare	Mandatory	-21,555,000,000
Premiums Collected for the Aged, FSMI Fund	Medicare	Mandatory	-60,969,000,000
Federal Contributions for Benefits, Prescription Drug Account, SMI	Medicare	Mandatory	-65,644,000,000
Federal Contributions, FSMI Fund	Medicare	Mandatory	-207,931,000,000
Total – Department of Health and Human Services			-410,077,000,000

Bureau of Economic Analysis Category HHS Budget Summary Department of Health and Human Services FY2015 Budget

Account Name	Sub-function Title	BEA Category	Budget
Health Resources and Services	Health care services	Discretionary	3,638,000,000
Health Resources and Services	Health care services	Discretionary	2,336,000,000
Primary Health Care Access	Health care services	Mandatory	2,167,000,000
Health Resources and Services	Health research and training	Discretionary	593,000,000
Maternal, Infant, and Early Childhood Home Visiting Programs	Health care services	Mandatory	389,000,000
Vaccine Injury Compensation Program Trust Fund	Health care services	Mandatory	249,000,000
Health Resources and Services	Health research and training	Mandatory	75,000,000
Vaccine Injury Compensation Program Trust Fund	Health care services	Discretionary	19,000,000
Health Resources and Services	Health care services	Mandatory	1,000,000
Health Education Assistance Loans Liquidating Account	Health research and training	Mandatory	-8,000,000
Total – Health Resources and Services Administration			9,459,000,000

Bureau of Economic Analysis Category
HHS Budget Summary
Indian Health Services
FY2015 Budget

Account Name	Sub-function Title	BEA Category	Budget
Indian Health Services	Health care services	Discretionary	4,007,000,000
Indian Health Facilities	Health care services	Discretionary	462,000,000
Indian Health Facilities	Health care services	Mandatory	8,000,000
Total – Indian Health Services			4,477,000,000

Bureau of Economic Analysis Category HHS Budget Summary National Institutes of Health FY2015 Budget

Account Name	Sub-function Title	BEA Category	Budget
National Institutes of Health	Health research and training	Discretionary	31,174,000,000
National Institutes of Health	Health research and training	Mandatory	131,000,000
Total – National Institutes of Health			31,305,000,000

Bureau of Economic Analysis Category
HHS Budget Summary
Office of the Inspector General
FY2015 Budget

Account Name	Sub-function Title	BEA Category	Budget
Retirement Pay and Medical Benefits for Commissioned Officers	Health care services	Discretionary	51,000,000
Total – Office of the Inspector General			51,000,000

Bureau of Economic Analysis Category
HHS Budget Summary
Program Support Center
FY2015 Budget

Account Name	Sub-function Title	BEA Category	Budget
Retirement Pay and Medical Benefits for Commissioned Officers	Health care services	Mandatory	647,000,000
Miscellaneous Trust Funds	Health care services	Mandatory	82,000,000
HHS Accrual Contribution to the Uniformed Services Retiree Health Care Fund	Health care services	Discretionary	34,000,000
Total – Program Support Center			763,000,000

Bureau of Economic Analysis Category
HHS Budget Summary
Substance Abuse and Mental Health Services
FY2015 Budget

Account Name	Sub-function Title	BEA Category	Budget
Substance Abuse and Mental Health Services	Health care services	Discretionary	2,848,000,000
Substance Abuse and Mental Health Services	Health care services	Discretionary	431,000,000
Total – Substance Abuse and Mental Health Services			3,279,000,000

Bureau of Economic Analysis Category
HHS Budget Summary
Account Name
FY2015 Budget

Account Name	Budget
Administration for Children and Families	50,724,000,000
Administration on Aging	2,450,000,000
Agency for Healthcare Research and Quality	132,000,000
Centers for Disease Control and Prevention	5,872,000,000
Centers for Medicare and Medicaid Services	1,343,554,000,000
Department of Health and Human Services	-410,077,000,000
Departmental Management	3,893,000,000
Food and Drug Administration	2,759,000,000
Health Resources and Services Administration	9,459,000,000
Indian Health Services	4,477,000,000
National Institutes of Health	31,305,000,000
Office of the Inspector General	51,000,000
Program Support Center	763,000,000
Substance Abuse and Mental Health Services Administration	3,279,000,000
Total HHS Summary by Account Name	1,048,641,000,000

Bureau of Economic Analysis Category
HHS Budget Summary
Sub-function Title
FY2015 Budget

Sub-function Title	Budget
Atomic energy defense activities	61,000,000
Consumer and occupational health and safety	2,756,000,000
Deductions for offsetting receipts	-56,000,000
Federal law enforcement activities	45,000,000
Health care services	397,987,000,000
Health research and training	32,077,000,000
Medicare	563,836,000,000
Other income security	38,119,000,000
Other interest	-155,000,000
Social services	13,971,000,000
Total – Sub-function Title	1,048,641,000,000

Bureau of Economic Analysis Category
HHS Budget Summary
BEA Category
FY2015 Budget

Sub-function Title	BEA Category	Budget
Consumer and occupational health and safety	Discretionary	2,754,000,000
Federal law enforcement activities	Discretionary	45,000,000
Health care services	Discretionary	21,905,000,000
Health research and training	Discretionary	31,936,000,000
Medicare	Discretionary	6,831,000,000
Other income security	Discretionary	6,154,000,000
Social services	Discretionary	11,674,000,000
Total Discretionary Programs	Percent of Total - 8%	81,299,000,000
Sub-function Title	BEA Category	Budget
Atomic energy defense activities	Mandatory	61,000,000
Consumer and occupational health and safety	Mandatory	2,000,000
Deductions for offsetting receipts	Mandatory	-56,000,000
Health care services	Mandatory	376,082,000,000
Health research and training	Mandatory	141,000,000
Medicare	Mandatory	557,005,000,000
Other income security	Mandatory	31,965,000,000
Social services	Mandatory	2,297,000,000
Other interest	Mandatory	-155,000,000
Total Mandatory Programs	Percent of Total - 92%	967,342,000,000

HHS Budget Summary
BEA Category Totals

BEA Category	Budget	Percent
Discretionary	81,299,000,000	8%
Mandatory	967,342,000,000	92%
Total	1,048,641,000,000	100%

Bureau of Economic Analysis Category Budget Analysis Department of Defense – Military Programs FY2015 Budget

Bureau Name	Account Name	Sub-function Title	BEA Category	Budget
Allowances	Other Legislation	Department of Defense-Military	Discretionary	44,685,000,000
Department of Defense--Military Programs	Deltas between the Annualized CR Amounts and the FY 2011 Budget Request	Department of Defense-Military	Discretionary	760,000,000
Department of Defense--Military Programs	Rent of Equipment and Other Personal Property	Department of Defense-Military	Mandatory	-1,000,000
Department of Defense--Military Programs	Sale of Certain Materials in National Defense Stockpile	Department of Defense-Military	Mandatory	-20,000,000
Department of Defense--Military Programs	Deposits for Survivor Annuity Benefits	Department of Defense-Military	Mandatory	-21,000,000
Department of Defense--Military Programs	Sale of Scrap and Salvage Materials	Department of Defense-Military	Mandatory	-1,000,000
Department of Defense--Military Programs	Recoveries for Government Property Lost or Damaged	Department of Defense-Military	Mandatory	-12,000,000
Department of Defense--Military Programs	Recoveries under the Foreign Military Sales Program, Navy	Department of Defense-Military	Mandatory	-156,000,000
Department of Defense--Military Programs	Recoveries under the Foreign Military Sales Program, Army	Department of Defense-Military	Mandatory	-22,000,000
Department of Defense--Military Programs	Recoveries under the Foreign Military Sales Program, Air Force	Department of Defense-Military	Mandatory	-41,000,000

Department of Defense--Military Programs	Recoveries under the Foreign Military Sales Program, Defense Bureaus	Department of Defense-Military	Mandatory	-5,000,000
Department of Defense--Military Programs	General Fund Proprietary Receipts, not Otherwise Classified, Navy	Department of Defense-Military	Mandatory	-82,000,000

Bureau of Economic Analysis Category Budget Analysis (Continued) Department of Defense – Military Programs FY2015 Budget

Department of Defense-- Military Programs	General Fund Proprietary Receipts, not Otherwise Classified, Army	Department of Defense-Military	Mandatory	-68,000,000
Department of Defense-- Military Programs	General Fund Proprietary Receipts, not Otherwise Classified, Air Force	Department of Defense-Military	Mandatory	-97,000,000
Department of Defense-- Military Programs	General Fund Proprietary Receipts, not Otherwise Classified, Defense Bureaus	Department of Defense-Military	Mandatory	-87,000,000
Department of Defense-- Military Programs	Undistributed Intra-governmental Payments and Receivables from Cancelled Accounts, Navy	Department of Defense-Military	Mandatory	-45,000,000
Department of Defense-- Military Programs	Restoration of the Rocky Mountain Arsenal, Army	Department of Defense-Military	Mandatory	-7,000,000
Department of Defense-- Military Programs	Overseas Military Facility, Investment and Recovery	Department of Defense-Military	Mandatory	-1,000,000
Department of Defense-- Military Programs	Proceeds from the Transfer or Disposition of Commissary Facilities	Department of Defense-Military	Mandatory	-1,000,000
Department of Defense-- Military Programs	Proceeds from the Transfer or Disposition of Commissary Facilities	Department of Defense-Military	Mandatory	-6,000,000
Department of Defense-- Military Programs	Contributions for Burden sharing and Other Cooperative Activities (Kuwait)	Department of Defense-Military	Mandatory	-177,000,000

Department of Defense--Military Programs	Contributions for Burden sharing and Other Cooperative Activities (Japan)	Department of Defense-Military	Mandatory	-266,000,000

Bureau of Economic Analysis Category Budget Analysis (Continued) Department of Defense – Military Programs FY2015 Budget

Department of Defense-- Military Programs	Contributions for Burden sharing and Other Cooperative Activities (So. Korea)	Department of Defense-Military	Mandatory	-414,000,000
Department of Defense-- Military Programs	Foreign National Employees Separation Pay Trust Fund	Department of Defense-Military	Mandatory	-44,000,000
Department of Defense-- Military Programs	Payment to Voluntary Separation Incentive Fund	Department of Defense-Military	Mandatory	-57,000,000
Department of Defense-- Military Programs	Disposal of Department of Defense Real Property	Department of Defense-Military	Mandatory	-13,000,000
Department of Defense-- Military Programs	Lease of Department of Defense Real Property	Department of Defense-Military	Mandatory	-17,000,000
Department of Defense-- Military Programs	Deposits, Other DOD Trust Funds	Department of Defense-Military	Mandatory	-5,000,000
Department of Defense-- Military Programs	Profits from Sale of Ships' Shores, Other DOD Trust Funds	Department of Defense-Military	Mandatory	-20,000,000
Total				-926,000,000

Bureau of Economic Analysis Category Budget Analysis (Continued) Department of Defense – Military Programs FY2015 Budget

Bureau Name	Account Name	Sub-function Title	BEA Category	Budget
Family Housing	Family Housing Construction, Army	Department of Defense-Military	Discretionary	211,000,000
Family Housing	Family Housing Construction, Army	Department of Defense-Military	Discretionary	543,000,000
Family Housing	Family Housing Construction, Army	Department of Defense-Military	Discretionary	159,000,000
Family Housing	Family Housing Construction, Army	Department of Defense-Military	Discretionary	359,000,000
Family Housing	Family Housing Construction, Army	Department of Defense-Military	Discretionary	212,000,000
Family Housing	Family Housing Construction, Army	Department of Defense-Military	Discretionary	326,000,000
Family Housing	Family Housing Construction, Army	Department of Defense-Military	Discretionary	50,000,000
Family Housing	Department of Defense Family Housing Improvement Fund	Department of Defense-Military	Discretionary	94,000,000
Total				1,954,000,000

Bureau of Economic Analysis Category Department of Defense – Military Programs (Continued) Military Construction FY2015 Budget

Bureau Name	Account Name	Sub-function Title	BEA Category	Budget
Military Construction	Chemical Demilitarization Construction, Defense-wide	Department of Defense-Military	Discretionary	96,000,000
Military Construction	Military Construction, Defense-wide	Department of Defense-Military	Discretionary	4,145,000,000
Military Construction	Department of Defense Base Closure Account 1990	Department of Defense-Military	Discretionary	339,000,000
Military Construction	Department of Defense Base Closure Account 2005	Department of Defense-Military	Discretionary	780,000,000
Military Construction	North Atlantic Treaty Organization Security Investment Program	Department of Defense-Military	Discretionary	270,000,000
Military Construction	Military Construction, Navy and Marine Corps	Department of Defense-Military	Discretionary	2,463,000,000
Military Construction	Military Construction, Navy Reserve	Department of Defense-Military	Discretionary	60,000,000
Military Construction	Military Construction, Army	Department of Defense-Military	Discretionary	4,474,000,000
Military Construction	Military Construction, Army National Guard	Department of Defense-Military	Discretionary	604,000,000
Military Construction	Military Construction, Army Reserve	Department of Defense-Military	Discretionary	336,000,000
Military Construction	Military Construction, Air Force	Department of Defense-Military	Discretionary	1,480,000,000
Military Construction	Military Construction, Air Force Reserve	Department of Defense-Military	Discretionary	45,000,000
Military Construction	Military Construction, Air National Guard	Department of Defense-Military	Discretionary	133,000,000
Total				15,225,000,000

Bureau of Economic Analysis Category Budget Analysis Department of Defense – Military Personnel FY2015 Budget

Bureau Name	Account Name	Sub-function Title	BEA Category	Budget
Military Personnel	Medicare-Eligible Retiree Health Fund Contribution, Navy	Department of Defense-Military	Discretionary	1,951,000,000
Military Personnel	Medicare-Eligible Retiree Health Fund Contribution, Navy	Department of Defense-Military	Discretionary	1,246,000,000
Military Personnel	Medicare-Eligible Retiree Health Fund Contribution, Navy	Department of Defense-Military	Discretionary	255,000,000
Military Personnel	Medicare-Eligible Retiree Health Fund Co	Department of Defense-Military	Discretionary	147,000,000
Military Personnel	Medicare-Eligible Retiree Health Fund Contribution, Navy	Department of Defense-Military	Discretionary	3,355,000,000
Military Personnel	Medicare-Eligible Retiree Health Fund Contribution, Navy	Department of Defense-Military	Discretionary	771,000,000
Military Personnel	Medicare-Eligible Retiree Health Fund Contribution, Navy	Department of Defense-Military	Discretionary	1,350,000,000
Military Personnel	Medicare-Eligible Retiree Health Fund Contribution, Navy	Department of Defense-Military	Discretionary	2,035,000,000
Military Personnel	Medicare-Eligible Retiree Health Fund Contribution, Navy	Department of Defense-Military	Discretionary	264,000,000
Military Personnel	Medicare-Eligible Retiree Health Fund Contribution, Navy	Department of Defense-Military	Discretionary	417,000,000
Military Personnel	Military Personnel, Marine Corps	Department of Defense-Military	Discretionary	14,092,000,000

Bureau Name	Account Name	Sub-function Title	BEA Category	Budget
Military Personnel	Reserve Personnel, Marine Corps	Department of Defense-Military	Discretionary	678,000,000
Military Personnel	Reserve Personnel, Navy	Department of Defense-Military	Discretionary	2,045,000,000
Military Personnel	Military Personnel, Navy	Department of Defense-Military	Discretionary	27,697,000,000
Military Personnel	Military Personnel, Army	Department of Defense-Military	Discretionary	45,370,000,000
Military Personnel	National Guard Personnel, Army	Department of Defense-Military	Discretionary	7,861,000,000
Military Personnel	Reserve Personnel, Army	Department of Defense-Military	Discretionary	4,511,000,000
Military Personnel	Military Personnel, Air Force	Department of Defense-Military	Discretionary	29,568,000,000
Military Personnel	Reserve Personnel, Air Force	Department of Defense-Military	Discretionary	1,836,000,000
Military Personnel	National Guard Personnel, Air Force	Department of Defense-Military	Discretionary	3,253,000,000
Military Personnel	Concurrent Receipt Accrual Payments to the Military Retirement Fund	Department of Defense-Military	Mandatory	5,475,000,000
Total				154,177,000,000

Bureau of Economic Analysis Category Budget Analysis
Department of Defense – Operation and Maintenance FY2015 Budget

Bureau Name	Account Name	Sub-function Title	BEA Category	Budget
Operation and Maintenance	Operation and Maintenance, Defense-wide	Department of Defense-Military	Discretionary	35,868,000,000
Operation and Maintenance	United States Court of Appeals for the Armed Forces	Department of Defense-Military	Discretionary	15,000,000
Operation and Maintenance	Drug Interdiction and Counter-Drug Activities	Department of Defense-Military	Discretionary	1,145,000,000
Operation and Maintenance	Office of the Inspector General	Department of Defense-Military	Discretionary	282,000,000
Operation and Maintenance	Department of Defense Acquisition Workforce Development Fund	Department of Defense-Military	Discretionary	298,000,000
Operation and Maintenance	Overseas Contingency Operations Transfer Fund	Department of Defense-Military	Discretionary	1,083,000,000
Operation and Maintenance	Defense Health Program	Department of Defense-Military	Discretionary	35,445,000,000
Operation and Maintenance	Cooperative Threat Reduction Account	Department of Defense-Military	Discretionary	470,000,000
Operation and Maintenance	The Department of Defense Environmental Restoration Accounts	Department of Defense-Military	Discretionary	1,151,000,000
Operation and Maintenance	Environmental Restoration, Formerly Used Defense Sites	Department of Defense-Military	Discretionary	280,000,000
Operation and Maintenance	Overseas Humanitarian, Disaster, and Civic Aid	Department of Defense-Military	Discretionary	137,000,000
Operation and Maintenance	Operation and Maintenance, Marine Corps	Department of Defense-Military	Discretionary	6,404,000,000
Operation and Maintenance	Operation and Maintenance, Marine Corps Reserve	Department of Defense-Military	Discretionary	284,000,000

Bureau Name	Account Name	Sub-function Title	BEA Category	Budget
Operation and Maintenance	Operation and Maintenance, Navy	Department of Defense-Military	Discretionary	40,258,000,000
Operation and Maintenance	Operation and Maintenance, Navy Reserve	Department of Defense-Military	Discretionary	1,306,000,000
Operation and Maintenance	Operation and Maintenance, Army	Department of Defense-Military	Discretionary	40,277,000,000
Operation and Maintenance	Operation and Maintenance, Army National Guard	Department of Defense-Military	Discretionary	7,303,000,000
Operation and Maintenance	Operation and Maintenance, Army Reserve	Department of Defense-Military	Discretionary	3,200,000,000
Operation and Maintenance	Afghanistan Security Forces Fund	Department of Defense-Military	Discretionary	646,000,000
Operation and Maintenance	Afghanistan Infrastructure Fund	Department of Defense-Military	Discretionary	19,000,000
Operation and Maintenance	Operation and Maintenance, Air Force	Department of Defense-Military	Discretionary	36,950,000,000
Operation and Maintenance	Operation and Maintenance, Air Force Reserve	Department of Defense-Military	Discretionary	3,314,000,000
Operation and Maintenance	Operation and Maintenance, Air National Guard	Department of Defense-Military	Discretionary	6,234,000,000
Operation and Maintenance	Disposal of Department of Defense Real Property	Department of Defense-Military	Discretionary	10,000,000
Operation and Maintenance	Lease of Department of Defense Real Property	Department of Defense-Military	Discretionary	10,000,000
Operation and Maintenance	Miscellaneous Special Funds	Department of Defense-Military	Mandatory	8,000,000
Operation and Maintenance	Allied Contributions and Cooperation Account	Department of Defense-Military	Mandatory	620,000,000
Total				223,154,000,000

Bureau of Economic Analysis Category Budget Analysis (Continued) Department of Defense – Procurement FY2015 Budget

Bureau Name	Account Name	Sub-function Title	BEA Category	Budget
Procurement	Mine Resistant Ambush Protected Vehicle Fund	Department of Defense-Military	Discretionary	320,000
Procurement	Procurement, Defense-wide	Department of Defense-Military	Discretionary	5,101,000
Procurement	Joint Urgent Operational Needs Fund	Department of Defense-Military	Discretionary	105,000
Procurement	National Guard and Reserve Equipment	Department of Defense-Military	Discretionary	380,000
Procurement	Defense Production Act Purchases	Department of Defense-Military	Discretionary	16,000
Procurement	Chemical Agents and Munitions Destruction, Defense	Department of Defense-Military	Discretionary	1,365,000
Procurement	Procurement, Marine Corps	Department of Defense-Military	Discretionary	2,356,000
Procurement	Aircraft Procurement, Navy	Department of Defense-Military	Discretionary	19,435,000
Procurement	Weapons Procurement, Navy	Department of Defense-Military	Discretionary	3,501,000
Procurement	Procurement of Ammunition, Navy and Marine Corps	Department of Defense-Military	Discretionary	1,044,000
Procurement	Shipbuilding and Conversion, Navy	Department of Defense-Military	Discretionary	15,023,000
Procurement	Other Procurement, Navy	Department of Defense-Military	Discretionary	6,434,000
Procurement	Aircraft Procurement, Army	Department of Defense-Military	Discretionary	7,076,000
Procurement	Missile Procurement, Army	Department of Defense-Military	Discretionary	1,575,000

Bureau Name	Account Name	Sub-function Title	BEA Category	Budget
Procurement	Procurement of Weapons and Tracked Combat Vehicles, Army	Department of Defense-Military	Discretionary	2,367,000
Procurement	Procurement of Ammunition, Army	Department of Defense-Military	Discretionary	2,049,000
Procurement	Other Procurement, Army	Department of Defense-Military	Discretionary	10,875,000
Procurement	Joint Improvised Explosive Device Defeat Fund	Department of Defense-Military	Discretionary	897,000
Procurement	Aircraft Procurement, Air Force	Department of Defense-Military	Discretionary	15,499,000
Procurement	Procurement of Ammunition, Air Force	Department of Defense-Military	Discretionary	696,000
Procurement	Missile Procurement, Air Force	Department of Defense-Military	Discretionary	5,840,000
Procurement	Other Procurement, Air Force	Department of Defense-Military	Discretionary	18,565,000
Total				120,519,000,000

Bureau of Economic Analysis Category Budget Analysis (Continued) Department of Defense – Research, Development, Test, and Evaluation FY2015 Budget

Bureau Name	Account Name	Sub-function Title	BEA Category	Budget
Research, Development, Test, and Evaluation	NNSA Program Support	Department of Defense-Military	Discretionary	464,000,000
Research, Development, Test, and Evaluation	Research, Development, Test and Evaluation, Defense-wide	Department of Defense-Military	Discretionary	19,630,000,000
Research, Development, Test, and Evaluation	Operational Test and Evaluation, Defense	Department of Defense-Military	Discretionary	195,000,000
Research, Development, Test, and Evaluation	Research, Development, Test and Evaluation, Navy	Department of Defense-Military	Discretionary	17,734,000,000
Research, Development, Test, and Evaluation	Research, Development, Test and Evaluation, Army	Department of Defense-Military	Discretionary	10,220,000,000
Research, Development, Test, and Evaluation	Research, Development, Test and Evaluation, Air Force	Department of Defense-Military	Discretionary	26,368,000,000
Research, Development, Test, and Evaluation	Research, Development, Test and Evaluation, Defense-wide	Department of Defense-Military	Mandatory	100,000,000
Total				74,711,000,000

Bureau of Economic Analysis Category Budget Analysis Department of Defense – Revolving and Management Funds FY2015 Budget

Bureau Name	Account Name	Sub-function Title	BEA Category	Budget
Revolving and Management Funds	National Defense Sealift Fund	Department of Defense-Military	Discretionary	1,258,000,000
Revolving and Management Funds	Working Capital Fund, Army	Department of Defense-Military	Discretionary	1,741,000,000
Revolving and Management Funds	Working Capital Fund, Navy	Department of Defense-Military	Discretionary	13,000,000
Revolving and Management Funds	Working Capital Fund, Air Force	Department of Defense-Military	Discretionary	66,000,000
Revolving and Management Funds	Working Capital Fund, Defense Commissary Agency	Department of Defense-Military	Discretionary	24,000,000
Revolving and Management Funds	Working Capital Fund, Defense-Wide	Department of Defense-Military	Discretionary	454,000,000
Revolving and Management Funds	National Defense Stockpile Transaction Fund	Department of Defense-Military	Mandatory	44,000,000
Revolving and Management Funds	Buildings Maintenance Fund	Department of Defense-Military	Mandatory	8,000,000
Revolving and Management Funds	Pentagon Reservation Maintenance Revolving Fund	Department of Defense-Military	Mandatory	13,000,000
Total				3,621,000,000

Bureau of Economic Analysis Category Budget Analysis Department of Defense – Trust Funds FY2015 Budget

Bureau Name	Account Name	Sub-function Title	BEA Category	Budget
Trust Funds	Foreign National Employees Separation Pay	Department of Defense-Military	Mandatory	44,000,000
Trust Funds	Voluntary Separation Incentive Fund	Department of Defense-Military	Mandatory	114,000,000
Trust Funds	Host Nation Support Fund for Relocation	Department of Defense-Military	Mandatory	239,000,000
Trust Funds	Other DOD Trust Funds	Department of Defense-Military	Mandatory	34,000,000
Total				431,000,000

Bureau of Economic Analysis Category Department of Defense – Military Programs (Continued) Bureau Name Summary FY2015 Budget

Bureau Name	Budget
Allowances	44,685,000,000
Department of Defense--Military Programs	-926,000,000
Family Housing	1,954,000,000
Military Construction	15,225,000,000
Military Personnel	154,177,000,000
Operation and Maintenance	223,154,000,000
Procurement	120,519,000,000
Research, Development, Test, and Evaluation	74,711,000,000
Revolving and Management Funds	3,621,000,000
Trust Funds	431,000,000
Total	637,551,000,000

Discretionary and Mandatory

Bureau Name	BEA Category	Budget
Allowances	Discretionary	44,685,000,000
Department of Defense--Military Programs	Discretionary	760,000,000
Family Housing	Discretionary	1,954,000,000
Military Construction	Discretionary	15,225,000,000
Military Personnel	Discretionary	148,702,000,000
Operation and Maintenance	Discretionary	222,526,000,000
Procurement	Discretionary	120,519,000,000
Research, Development, Test, and Evaluation	Discretionary	74,611,000,000
Revolving and Management Funds	Discretionary	3,556,000,000
Total		632,538,000,000
Bureau Name	BEA Category	Budget
Department of Defense--Military Programs	Mandatory	-1,686,000,000
Military Personnel	Mandatory	5,475,000,000
Operation and Maintenance	Mandatory	628,000,000
Research, Development, Test, and Evaluation	Mandatory	100,000,000
Revolving and Management Funds	Mandatory	65,000,000
Trust Funds	Mandatory	431,000,000
Total		5,013,000,000

Bureau of Economic Analysis Category Social Security Administration FY2015 Budget

Bureau Name	Account Name	Sub-function Title	BEA Category	Budget
Social Security Administration	Social Security Administration	Income security for veterans	Discretionary	1,000,000
Social Security Administration	Social Security Administration	Income security for veterans	Mandatory	6,000,000
Social Security Administration	Social Security Administration	Other income security	Discretionary	3,759,000,000
Social Security Administration	Social Security Administration	Other income security	Mandatory	51,460,000,000
Social Security Administration	Social Security Administration	Social security	Discretionary	6,501,000,000
Social Security Administration	Social Security Administration	Social security	Mandatory	846,495,000,000
Total				908,222,000,000

Social Security Administration

Sub-function Title	BEA Category	Budget
Income security for veterans	Discretionary	1,000,000
Other income security	Discretionary	3,759,000,000
Social security	Discretionary	6,501,000,000
Total Discretionary		10,261,000,000
Sub-function Title	BEA Category	Budget
Income security for veterans	Mandatory	6,000,000
Other income security	Mandatory	51,460,000,000
Social security	Mandatory	846,495,000,000
Total Mandatory		897,961,000,000
Total Budget		908,222,000,000

Bureau of Economic Analysis Category
Department of the Treasury
Budget Summary
FY2015 Budget

Bureau Name	Sub-function Title	BEA Category	Budget
Alcohol and Tobacco Tax and Trade Bureau	Central fiscal operations	Discretionary	93,000,000
Alcohol and Tobacco Tax and Trade Bureau	General purpose fiscal assistance	Mandatory	425,000,000
Bureau of the Public Debt	Central fiscal operations	Discretionary	159,000,000
Bureau of the Public Debt	Central fiscal operations	Mandatory	131,000,000
Comptroller of the Currency	Assessment Funds	Mandatory	-44,000,000
Department of the Treasury	Mortgage credit	Mandatory	-16,738,000,000
Department of the Treasury	Other advancement of commerce	Mandatory	-32,000,000
Department of the Treasury	General retirement and disability insurance (excluding social security)	Mandatory	-246,000,000
Department of the Treasury	Federal litigative and judicial activities	Mandatory	-10,000,000
Department of the Treasury	Central fiscal operations	Discretionary	1,000,000
Department of the Treasury	Central fiscal operations	Mandatory	-1,434,000,000
Department of the Treasury	Other general government	Mandatory	-3,000,000
Department of the Treasury	Deductions for offsetting receipts	Mandatory	-510,000,000
Department of the Treasury	Other interest	Net interest	-77,003,000,000
Departmental Offices	International financial programs	Mandatory	-302,000,000
Departmental Offices	Energy supply	Mandatory	1,841,000,000
Departmental Offices	Mortgage credit	Mandatory	14,000,000
Departmental Offices	Other advancement of commerce	Discretionary	45,000,000
Departmental Offices	Other advancement of Commerce	Mandatory	795,000,000

Departmental Offices	Community development	Discretionary	219,000,000
Departmental Offices	Housing assistance	Mandatory	5,134,000,000
Departmental Offices	Federal law enforcement activities	Mandatory	800,000,000
Departmental Offices	Central fiscal operations	Discretionary	496,000,000
Departmental Offices	Other interest	Net interest	-430,000,000
Federal Financing Bank	Central fiscal operations	Mandatory	-464,000,000
Financial Crimes Enforcement Network	Federal law enforcement activities	Discretionary	109,000,000
Financial Management Service	Other natural resources	Mandatory	2,000,000
Financial Management Service	Central fiscal operations	Discretionary	211,000,000
Financial Management Service	Central fiscal operations	Mandatory	1,014,000,000
Total			725,673,000,000

Bureau of Economic Analysis Category Budget Summary Department of Veterans Affairs FY2015 Budget

Bureau Name	Budget
Benefits Programs	81,420,000,000
Department of Veterans Affairs	-3,563,000,000
Departmental Administration	7,737,000,000
Veterans Health Administration	57,217,000,000
Total	142,811,000,000

Discretionary and Mandatory

Bureau Name	BEA Category	Budget
Benefits Programs	Discretionary	165,000,000
Department of Veterans Affairs	Discretionary	-3,341,000,000
Departmental Administration	Discretionary	7,737,000,000
Veterans Health Administration	Discretionary	57,178,000,000
Total		61,739,000,000
Bureau Name	BEA Category	Budget
Benefits Programs	Mandatory	81,255,000,000
Department of Veterans Affairs	Mandatory	-215,000,000
Departmental Administration	Mandatory	0
Veterans Health Administration	Mandatory	39,000,000
Veterans Health Administration	Net Interest	-7,000,000
Total		81,072,000,000

Bureau of Economic Analysis Category Budget Summary Executive Office of the President FY2015 Budget

Bureau Name	Account Name	Sub-function Title	BEA Category	Budget
Council on Environmental Quality and Office of Environmental Quality	Council on Environmental Quality and Office of Environmental Quality	Executive direction and management	Discretionary	2,000,000
Unanticipated Needs	Integrated, Efficient and Effective Uses of Information Technology	Executive direction and management	Discretionary	58,000,000
Office of Management and Budget	Office of Management and Budget	Executive direction and management	Discretionary	89,000,000
Office of National Drug Control Policy	Office of National Drug Control Policy	Executive direction and management	Discretionary	22,000,000
Office of Science and Technology Policy	Office of Science and Technology Policy	Executive direction and management	Discretionary	6,000,000
Office of the United States Trade Representative	Office of the United States Trade Representative	Executive direction and management	Discretionary	49,000,000
Executive Residence at the White House	Operating Expenses	Executive direction and management	Discretionary	13,000,000
Unanticipated Needs	Partnership Fund for Program Integrity Innovation	Executive direction and management	Discretionary	19,000,000
Council of Economic Advisers	Salaries and Expenses	Executive direction and management	Discretionary	4,000,000
National Security Council and Homeland Security Council	Salaries and Expenses	Executive direction and management	Discretionary	13,000,000

Bureau Name	Account Name	Sub-function Title	BEA Category	Budget
Office of Administration	Salaries and Expenses	Executive direction and management	Discretionary	111,000,000
Special Assistance to the President and the Official Residence of the Vice President	Special Assistance to the President and the Official Residence of the Vice President	Executive direction and management	Discretionary	5,000,000
Unanticipated Needs	Spectrum Relocation Fund	Other advancement of commerce	Mandatory	100,000,000
The White House	The White House	Executive direction and management	Discretionary	57,000,000
Executive Residence at the White House	White House Repair and Restoration	Executive direction and management	Discretionary	1,000,000
Total				549,000,000

Bureau of Economic Analysis Category Budget Summary Other Defense Civil Programs FY2015 Budget

Bureau Name	Sub-function Title	Budget
American Battle Monuments Commission	Other veterans benefits and services	74,000,000
Armed Forces Retirement Home	Federal employee retirement and disability	55,000,000
Cemeterial Expenses	Other veterans benefits and services	44,000,000
Educational Benefits	Veterans education, training, and rehabilitation	510,000,000
Education Benefits	Veterans education, training, and rehabilitation	-384,000,000
Forest and Wildlife Conservation, Military Reservations	Recreational resources	1,000,000
Military Retirement	Defense-related activities	0
Military Retirement	Federal employee retirement and disability	55,502,000,000
Retiree Health Care	Defense-related activities	0
Retiree Health Care	Health care services	11,518,000,000
Retiree Health Care	Other interest	-8,183,000,000
Selective Service System	Defense-related activities	23,000,000
Total		59,160,000,000

Government Receipts
Fiscal Year 2014

Bureau Name	Source Category Name	Budget
Affordable Housing Program	Misc. Governmental Receipts	287,000,000
Bureau of Consumer Financial Protection	Misc. Governmental Receipts	544,000,000
Corporation for Travel Promotion	Misc. Governmental Receipts	100,000,000
Corps of Engineers--Civil Works	Duties, Taxes, and Gov. Receipts	1,662,000,000
Department of Agriculture	Duties, Taxes, and Gov. Receipts	12,341,000,000
Department of Commerce	Misc. Governmental Receipts	15,000,000
Department of Defense--Military Programs	Misc. Governmental Receipts	127,000,000
Department of Energy	Misc. Governmental Receipts	4,000,000
Department of Health and Human Services	Taxes, Receipts, and Social Insurance Taxes and Contributions	223,813,000,000
Department of Homeland Security	Duties, Taxes, and Gov. Receipts	1,718,000,000
Department of Justice	Misc. Governmental Receipts	5,093,000,000
Department of Labor	Taxes, Receipts, and Social Insurance Taxes and Contributions	60,964,000,000
Department of State	Receipts and Social Insurance Taxes and Contributions	724,000,000
Department of the Interior	Duties, Taxes, and Gov. Receipts	872,000,000
Department of the Treasury	Excise Taxes and Misc. Governmental Receipts	97,115,000,000
Department of Transportation	Excise Taxes	51,365,000,000
District of Columbia Courts	Social Insurance Taxes and Contributions	1,000,000
Electric Reliability Organization	Misc. Governmental Receipts	100,000,000
Environmental Protection Agency	Excise Taxes and Misc. Governmental Receipts	182,000,000
Federal Communications Commission	Misc. Governmental Receipts	9,756,000,000
Federal Deposit Insurance Corporation, activities	Misc. Governmental Receipts	158,000,000

Bureau Name	Source Category Name	Budget
Federal Financial Institutions Examination Council	Misc. Governmental Receipts	3,000,000
Federal Housing Finance Agency	Misc. Governmental Receipts	248,000,000
Governmental Receipts	Corporation Income Taxes	332,740,000,000
Governmental Receipts	Customs Duties	22,625,000,000
Governmental Receipts	Estate and Gift Taxes	15,746,000,000
Governmental Receipts	Excise Taxes	34,644,000,000
Governmental Receipts	Individual Income Taxes	1,386,068,000,000
Judicial Branch	Receipts and Social Insurance Taxes and Contributions	224,000,000
Library of Congress	Misc. Governmental Receipts	5,000,000
Office of Personnel Management	Social Insurance Taxes and Contributions	3,722,000,000
Armed Forces Retirement Home	Receipts and Social Insurance Taxes and Contributions	40,000,000
Patient-Centered Outcomes Research Trust Fund	Excise Taxes	347,000,000
Public Company Accounting Oversight Board	Misc. Governmental Receipts	241,000,000
Railroad Retirement Board	Social Insurance Taxes and Contributions	5,149,000,000
Securities and Exchange Commission	Misc.	50,000,000
Securities Investor Protection Corporation	Misc. Governmental Receipts	400,000,000
Social Security Administration	Social Insurance Taxes and Contributions	732,332,000,000
Standard Setting Body	Misc. Governmental Receipts	38,000,000
United Mine Workers of America Benefit Funds	Misc. Governmental Receipts	30,000,000
Total		3,001,593,000,000

Budget Summary
Designated Retirement Funds

Agency Name	Collections	Payments	Net Fund
Dept. of State	-24,000,000	1,008,000,000	984,000,000
Office of Personnel Mgmt.	-1,934,000,000	81,106,000,000	79,172,000,000
Federal Retirement Thrift Investment Board	-139,000,000	139,000,000	0
Other Defense Civil Programs	-12,000,000	55,569,000,000	55,557,000,000
Dept. of Labor	0	363,000,000	363,000,000
International Assistance Programs	-4,000,000	4,000,000	0
Judicial Branch	0	89,000,000	89,000,000
Legislative Branch	0	1,000,000	1,000,000
District of Columbia	0	9,000,000	9,000,000
Railroad Retirement Board	-7,981,000,000	14,792,000,000	6,811,000,000
Total	-10,094,000,000	153,080,000,000	142,986,000,000

Budget Summary
Social Security and Medicare

Agency Name	Contributions	Payments	Net Budget
Social Security Administration	-38,782,000,000	947,004,000,000	908,222,000,000
Medicare	-398,712,000,000	962,548,000,000	563,836,000,000
Total	-437,494,000,000	1,909,552,000,000	1,472,058,000,000

Budget Summary
Total Retirement and Medicare

Programs	Contributions	Payments	Total
Total Retirement, Social Security and Medicare	-447,588,000,000	2,062,632,000,000	1,615,044,000,000
Total Budget	-1,103,825,000,000	5,080,966,000,000	3,977,141,000,000
Percent of Total Budget	40.5%	40.6%	40.6%

Potential Budget Reductions in Discretionary Spending Fiscal Year 2015

Department	Mandatory Programs	Discretionary Programs	Total Budget
Legislative Branch	133,000,000	4,847,000,000	4,980,000,000
Judicial Branch	719,000,000	6,618,000,000	7,337,000,000
Agriculture	103,654,000,000	25,201,000,000	128,855,000,000
Commerce	1,600,000,000	9,033,000,000	10,633,000,000
Defense-Military Programs	5,062,000,000	639,015,000,000	644,077,000,000
Health and Human Services	1,037,666,000,000	80,102,000,000	1,117,768,000,000
Interior	-91,000,000	12,005,000,000	11,914,000,000
Justice	3,227,000,000	27,446,000,000	30,673,000,000
Labor	59,571,000,000	12,468,000,000	72,039,000,000
State	1,003,000,000	28,558,000,000	29,561,000,000
Treasury	817,525,000,000	16,039,000,000	833,564,000,000
Social Security Administration	91,820,000,000	3,796,000,000	95,616,000,000
Social Security Administration	855,313,000,000	6,618,000,000	861,931,000,000
Education	370,000,000	75,372,000,000	75,742,000,000
Energy	-1,660,000,000	31,636,000,000	29,976,000,000
Environmental Protection Agency	-239,000,000	7,867,000,000	7,628,000,000
Transportation	80,128,000,000	19,209,000,000	99,337,000,000
General Services Administration	-43,000,000	790,000,000	747,000,000
Homeland Security	922,000,000	44,915,000,000	45,837,000,000
Housing and Urban Development	-1,708,000,000	43,418,000,000	41,710,000,000
National Aeronautical and Space Administration	-14,000,000	18,054,000,000	18,040,000,000
Office of Personnel Management	90,812,000,000	254,000,000	91,066,000,000
Small Business Administration	0	874,000,000	874,000,000
Veterans Affairs	86,753,000,000	63,577,000,000	150,330,000,000
Executive Office of the President	100,000,000	449,000,000	549,000,000
Federal Drug Programs	0	332,000,000	332,000,000

Department	Mandatory Programs	Discretionary Programs	Total Budget
International Assistance Programs	-921,000,000	26,238,000,000	25,317,000,000
Other Defense Civil Programs	60,435,000,000	210,000,000	60,645,000,000
Corps of Engineers – Civil Works	83,000,000	4,976,000,000	5,059,000,000
Administrative Conference of the United States	0	3,000,000	3,000,000
Advisory Council on Historic Preservation	0	6,000,000	6,000,000
Appalachian Regional Commission	0	73,000,000	73,000,000
Access Board	0	7,000,000	7,000,000
Barry Goldwater Scholarship and Excellence in Education Foundation	4,000,000	0	4,000,000
Central Intelligence Agency	514,000,000	0	514,000,000
Commission of Fine Arts	0	2,000,000	2,000,000
Commission on Civil Rights	0	9,000,000	9,000,000
Committee for Purchase from People Who Are Blind or Severely Disabled	0	6,000,000	6,000,000
Commodity Futures Trading Commission	0	229,000,000	229,000,000
Consumer Product Safety Commission	0	112,000,000	112,000,000
Corporation for Public Broadcasting	0	457,000,000	457,000,000
United States Court of Appeals for Veterans Claims	4,000,000	54,000,000	58,000,000
Defense Nuclear Facilities Safety Board	0	28,000,000	28,000,000
District of Columbia	452,000,000	447,000,000	899,000,000
Equal Employment Opportunity Commission	-4,000,000	373,000,000	369,000,000
Export-Import Bank of the United States	-25,000,000	-282,000,000	-307,000,000
Farm Credit System Insurance Corporation	0	-281,000,000	-281,000,000
Federal Communications Commission	9,788,000,000	0	9,788,000,000

Department	Mandatory Programs	Discretionary Programs	Total Budget
Federal Deposit Insurance Corporation	-8,235,000,000	0	-8,235,000,000
Federal Election Commission	0	65,000,000	65,000,000
Federal Financial Institutions Examination Council		2,000,000	2,000,000
Federal Labor Relations Authority	0	25,000,000	25,000,000
Federal Maritime Commission	-1,000,000	25,000,000	24,000,000
Federal Mediation and Conciliation Service	0	46,000,000	46,000,000
Federal Mine Safety and Health Review Commission		21,000,000	21,000,000
Federal Retirement Thrift Investment Board	0	0	0
Federal Trade Commission	-10,000,000	189,000,000	179,000,000
Harry S Truman Scholarship Foundation	3,000,000	0	3,000,000
Institute of American Indian and Alaska Native Culture and Arts Development	0	9,000,000	9,000,000
United States Interagency Council on Homelessness	0	4,000,000	4,000,000
International Trade Commission	0	94,000,000	94,000,000
James Madison Memorial Fellowship Foundation	2,000,000	0	2,000,000
Japan-United States Friendship Commission	3,000,000	0	3,000,000
Legal Services Corporation	0	435,000,000	435,000,000
Marine Mammal Commission	0	3,000,000	3,000,000
Merit Systems Protection Board	0	40,000,000	40,000,000
National Archives and Records Administration	-3,000,000	391,000,000	388,000,000
National Capital Planning Commission	0	8,000,000	8,000,000
National Council on Disability	0	3,000,000	3,000,000
National Credit Union Administration	-1,433,000,000	1,000,000	-1,432,000,000
National Endowment for the Arts	0	145,000,000	145,000,000

Department	Mandatory Programs	Discretionary Programs	Total Budget
National Endowment for the Humanities	0	144,000,000	144,000,000
National Labor Relations Board	0	278,000,000	278,000,000
National Mediation Board	0	14,000,000	14,000,000
National Science Foundation	321,000,000	7,305,000,000	7,626,000,000
National Transportation Safety Board	0	99,000,000	99,000,000
Neighborhood Reinvestment Corporation	0	207,000,000	207,000,000
Nuclear Regulatory Commission	-1,000,000	122,000,000	121,000,000
Nuclear Waste Technical Review Board	0	3,000,000	3,000,000
Occupational Safety and Health Review Commission	0	13,000,000	13,000,000
Office of Government Ethics	0	14,000,000	14,000,000
Office of Navajo and Hopi Indian Relocation	0	10,000,000	10,000,000
Office of Special Counsel	0	18,000,000	18,000,000
Postal Service	-536,000,000	328,000,000	-208,000,000
Railroad Retirement Board	6,888,000,000	164,000,000	7,052,000,000
Securities and Exchange Commission	-168,000,000	-1,000,000	-169,000,000
Smithsonian Institution	0	1,019,000,000	1,019,000,000
State Justice Institute	0	5,000,000	5,000,000
Tennessee Valley Authority	0	421,000,000	421,000,000
United States Holocaust Memorial Museum	0	51,000,000	51,000,000
United States Institute of Peace	0	49,000,000	49,000,000
Christopher Columbus Fellowship Foundation	0	1,000,000	1,000,000
Intelligence Community Management Account	0	579,000,000	579,000,000
Institute of Museum and Library Services	0	233,000,000	233,000,000
United Mine Workers of America Benefit Funds	26,000,000	0	26,000,000

Department	Mandatory Programs	Discretionary Programs	Total Budget
Corporation for National and Community Service	20,000,000	1,223,000,000	1,243,000,000
United States Enrichment Corporation Fund	-68,000,000	0	-68,000,000
Morris K. Udall and Stewart L. Udall Foundation	0	6,000,000	6,000,000
Other Commissions and Boards	0	1,000,000	1,000,000
Chemical Safety and Hazard Investigation Board	0	11,000,000	11,000,000
Court Services and Offender Supervision Agency for the District of Columbia	0	250,000,000	250,000,000
Presidio Trust	0	11,000,000	11,000,000
Denali Commission	0	16,000,000	16,000,000
Broadcasting Board of Governors	0	826,000,000	826,000,000
Delta Regional Authority	0	13,000,000	13,000,000
Vietnam Education Foundation	-5,000,000	0	-5,000,000
Election Assistance Corporation	0	11,000,000	11,000,000
Public Company Accounting Oversight Board	244,000,000	1,000,000	245,000,000
Standard Setting Body	47,000,000	0	47,000,000
Affordable Housing Program	216,000,000	0	216,000,000
Electric Reliability Organization	100,000,000	0	100,000,000
Office of the Federal Coordinator for Alaska Natural Gas Transportation Projects	0	4,000,000	4,000,000
Privacy and Civil Liberties Oversight Board	0	2,000,000	2,000,000
Federal Housing Finance Agency	247,000,000	-3,000,000	244,000,000
Recovery Accountability and Transparency Board	0	31,000,000	31,000,000
Northern Border Regional Commission	0	2,000,000	2,000,000
National Railroad Passenger Corporation Office of Inspector General	0	21,000,000	21,000,000
Securities Investor Protection	-22,000,000	0	-22,000,000

Department	Mandatory Programs	Discretionary Programs	Total Budget
Corporation			
Patient-Centered Outcomes Research Trust Fund	492,000,000	0	492,000,000
Corporation for Travel Promotion	100,000,000	0	100,000,000
Bureau of Consumer Financial Protection		448,000,000	448,000,000
Civilian Property Realignment Board	0	-3,744,000,000	-3,744,000,000
Allowances	-23,072,000,000	0	-23,072,000,000
Undistributed Offsetting Receipts	-308,519,000,000	-2,688,000,000	-311,207,000,000
Total	2,969,589,000,000	1,220,184,000,000	4,189,773,000,000

CHAPTER 8

THE FEDERAL BUDGET USING A STATEMENT OF CASH FLOW FINANCIAL STATEMENT FORMAT

The format used for this statement is mandated by Generally Accepted Accounting Principles (GAAP) for inclusion in audit reports and for public reporting of financial position and results of operations. The Federal Accounting Standards Board (FASB) has recently mandated that all government entities adopt the GAAP format for reporting to the public. The Statement of Cash Flow format presently used by the U.S. Government does not comply with the new format as required by the FASB. The Statement of Cash Flow presented on the following page is in compliance with both GAAP and FASB standards.

The following Statement of Cash Flow reflects an attempt to assign bureaus to the three activities within the Statement of Cash Flow. The assignments are a 'best guess' and are not presumed to be completely accurate. There are possibly expenditures in each activity that should be classified to a different activity. Without significant detail within each agency, it is not possible to be completely accurate.

The Government version of Cash Flow is titled 'Statement of Changes in Cash Balance'. The Government's version is too technical and too difficult to understand.

The Statement of Cash Flow provides enough detail to accommodate understanding. The budget deficit for both years is easily recognized and promotes a better understanding of the components of the budget deficits. Interest on the federal debt is reflected in 'Financing Activities' and is correctly presented as opposed to the Government version that misrepresents transactions through the Treasury Department.

Statement of Cash Flow
Budgets FY2015 and FY2014

	2015	2014
Cash Flow from Taxation		
Individual income taxes	1,498,000,000,000	1,383,000,000,000
Corporate income taxes	412,000,000,000	333,000,000,000
Other taxes	1,341,000,000,000	1,318,000,000,000
Total Cash Flow from Taxation	3,251,000,000,000	3,034,000,000,000
Less: Cash Flow used for Operating Activities		
Executive branch	549,000,000	549,000,000
Legislative branch	4,980,000,000	5,025,000,000
Judicial branch	7,337,000,000	7,275,000,000
Defense	644,077,000,000	637,550,000,000
Commerce	10,663,000,000	10,672,000,000
Health and Human Services	1,117,768,000,000	1,048,641,000,000
Homeland Security	45,837,000,000	33,428,000,000
Agriculture	128,855,000,000	136,675,000,000
Education	75,742,000,000	69,878,000,000
Labor	72,039,000,000	76,699,000,000
State	29,561,000,000	30,649,000,000
Veterans Affairs	150,330,000,000	142,811,000,000
District of Columbia	899,000,000	898,000,000

Environmental Protection Agency	7,628,000,000	7,349,000,000
Numerous Agencies and Others	876,935,000,000	848,344,000,000
Total Operating Activities	3,173,200,000,000	3,056,443,000,000
Less: Cash Flow used for Investing Activities		
Transportation	99,337,000,000	97,432,000,000
Energy	29,561,000,000	31,027,000,000
Housing and Urban Development	41,710,000,000	43,609,000,000
General Services Administration	747,000,000	860,000,000
Interior	11,914,000,000	12,127,000,000
Total Investing Activities	183,269,000,000	185,055,000,000

Less: Cash Flow used for Financing Activities		
Treasury	833,564,000,000	725,673,000,000
Cash Flow for Financing Activities	833,564,000,000	725,673,000,000
Total Cash Flow for all Activities	4,190,033,000,000	3,967,171,000,000
Budget (Deficit)	(939,033,000,000)	(933,171,000,000)

United States Government Statements of Changes in Cash Balance from Unified Budget and Other Activities for the Years Ended September 30, 2011 and 2010		
(In billions of dollars)	2011	2010

United States Government Statements of Changes in Cash Balance from Unified Budget and Other Activities for the Years Ended September 30, 2011 and 2010				
(In billions of dollars)	2011		2010	
Unified budget deficit		(1,298.6)		(1,294.1)
Adjustments for noncash outlays included in the budget:				
Interest accrued by Treasury on debt held by the public	244.2		206.8	
TARP yearend re-estimate	(46.9)		(86.4)	
TARP Subsidy expense/(income) (Note 5)	7.2		(24.2)	
Other Federal entity subsidy expense/(income) (Note 4)	(43.9)		(9.4)	
Subtotal		160.6		86.8
Items affecting the cash balance not included in the Budget:				
Net Transactions from financing activity:				
Borrowings from the public	7,962.8		8,525.5	
Repayment of debt held by the public	(6,854.2)		(7,054.5)	
Agency securities	1.0		0.7	
Subtotal		1,109.6		1,471.7
Transactions from monetary and other activity:				
Interest paid by Treasury on debt held by the public	(239.7)		(201.2)	
Net TARP direct loans and equity investments activity	59.0		111.8	
Net GSE—mortgage-backed securities activity	93.7		9.1	
Net loan receivable activity	(157.6)		(160.3)	
Allocations of special drawing rights	0.2		(1.0)	
Other	21.2		12.6	
Subtotal		(223.2)		(229.0)

United States Government Statements of Changes in Cash Balance from Unified Budget and Other Activities for the Years Ended September 30, 2011 and 2010				
(In billions of dollars)	2011		2010	
Cash and other monetary assets (Note 2):				
(Decrease)/increase in cash and other monetary assets		(251.6)		35.4
Balance, beginning of period		428.6		393.2
Balance, end of period		177.0		428.6

Maybe you can explain this...I can't.

Definition of Free Cash Flow

Operating Cash Flow (Taxes less Operating Activities less Investing Activities (Capital Assets) = Free Cash Flow

Free Cash Flow is cash that is available to pay interest and principal on the federal debt. The calculation of Free Cash Flow illustrates the proper or improper use of cash flow for purposes other than funding operations or increasing the asset base. If Free Cash Flow is negative it indicates improper use of financing activities (long-term borrowing). Continued negative Free Cash Flow could indicate long term problems and the inability to continue effective operations without some form of restructuring, either debt or operations.

Free Cash Flow	2016	2015	2014	2013
Tax Receipts	3,567,952,000,000	3,337,425,000,000	3,001,721,000,000	2,775,103,000,000
Less: Operating Activities	2,068,636,000,000	2,275,752,000,000	2,411,345,000,000	2,336,831,000,000
Less: Investing Activities	305,184,000,000	320,847,000,000	350,903,000,000	325,047,000,000
Free Cash Flow	1,194,132,000,000	740,826,000,000	239,473,000,000	113,225,000,000

Free Cash Flow	2012	2011	2010	2009
Tax Receipts	2,450,164,000,000	2,303,406,000,000	2,162,706,000,000	2,104,989,000,000
Less: Operating Activities	2,409,986,000,000	2,557,345,000,000	2,681,249,000,000	2,850,445,000,000
Less: Investing Activities	310,903,000,000	300,483,000,000	300,053,000,000	305,434,000,000

Free Cash Flow	-229,711,000,000	-554,362,000,000	-818,596,000,000	-1,050,890,000,000

Year	Result of Free Cash Flow	Principal Due	Interest Expense	Net Cash Flow
2016	1,194,132,000,000			
5/2015	482,272,000,000	4,265,436,000,000	257,730,000,000	-5,005,438,000,000
2014	239,473,000,000	6,676,502,000,000	437,682,000,000	-6,874,711,000,000
2013	113,225,000,000	7,482,227,000,000	428,126,000,000	-7,797,128,000,000
2012	-229,711,000,000	6,619,330,000,000	431,753,000,000	-7,280,794,000,000
2011	-554,362,000,000	6,860,979,000,000	450,099,000,000	-7,865,440,000,000
2010	-818,596,000,000	7,062,430,000,000	401,850,000,000	-8,282,876,000,000
2009	-1,050,890,000,000	7,202,840,000,000	363,830,000,000	-8,617,560,000,000

The 'Net Cash Flow' column illustrates the cash Crisis that has existed since 2009. The negative cash flow is solved by additional borrowings on the federal debt. Without significant budget cuts the negative cash flow will continue until treasury securities are no longer considered a good investment.

Operating Activities (000)

Operating Activities	2009 (000)	2010 (000)	2011 (000)	2012 (000)	2013 (000)	2014 (000)	2015 (000)	2016 (000)
Legislative	4,704	5,839	4,919	5,333	5,185	5,025	4,980	5,075
Judicial	6,645	7,181	7,370	7,567	7,278	7,275	7,337	7,476
Agriculture	114,440	129,460	152,085	144,008	145,227	136,675	128,855	126,903
Commerce	10,718	13,236	11,885	13,141	11,003	10,672	10,633	10,822
Defense INVESTING								
HHS	796,267	854,059	909,713	892,700	944,668	1,048,641	1,117,768	1,208,597
Interior INVESTING								
Justice INVESTING								
Labor	138,157	173,053	148,011	109,017	83,192	76,699	72,039	70,030
State	21,427	23,802	28,890	32,480	31,829	30,649	29,561	29,538
Treasury FINANCING								
SSA	727,549	754,178	801,436	814,908	861,647	908,222	957,547	1,015,005
Education	53,389	92,858	79,363	70,907	67,266	69,878	75,742	81,233
Energy INVESTING								
EPA	8,070	11,007	11,100	9,986	7,269	7,349	7,628	7,860
Transportation INVESTING								
Homeland Security INVESTING								
HUD INVESTING								
OPM	72,302	69,915	80,619	80,125	83,725	87,255	91,066	94,453
SBA	2,246	6,128	6,218	1,205	942	878	874	890
Veterans Affairs	95,457	108,274	141,130	124,325	134,867	142,811	150,330	163,808
Executive Office	743	582	463	574	558	549	549	561

Federal Drug Control	395	366	384	389	360	347	332	336
IAP	14,797	20,041	25,161	29,399	24,255	23,728	25,317	27,166
Other Defense INVESTING								
District of Columbia	908	955	947	953	914	898	899	902
Postal Service	422	4,818	1,651	-186	-199	-206	-208	-210
Total Operating Activities	2,068,636	2,275,752	2,411,345	2,336,831	2,409,986	2,557,345	2,681,249	2,850,445

Investing Activities

Investing Activities	2009 (000)	2010 (000)	2011 (000)	2012 (000)	2013 (000)	2014 (000)	2015 (000)	2016 (000)
Defense	149,553	157,945	176,265	156,298	145,026	137,698	137,612	140,541
Interior	4,627	5,092	5,002	4,908	4,694	4,684	4,763	4,918
Justice	6,009	6,327	6,421	6,951	6,585	6,541	6,588	6,730
Energy	17,141	23,891	36,529	31,355	24,875	20,693	19,224	18,343
Transportation	73,004	77,750	79,495	89,622	94,937	97,432	99,337	102,278,
GSA	254	790	2,279	1,702	1,009	595	479	374
Homeland Security	12,123	11,376	12,682	12,182	12,303	12,691	13,094	13,511
HUD	16,262	8,361	1,977	-4,363	-3,810	-3,656	-4,273	-4,698
NASA	19,168	18,906	19,477	18,174	18,312	18,032	18,040	18,326
Other Defense	201	173	141	203	139	129	130	133
Corp of Engineers	6,842	9,876	10,635	8,015	6,833	5,644	5,059	4,978
Total Investing Activities	305,184	320,487	350,903	325,047	310,903	300,483	300,053	305,434

APPENDICES

A. Percentage increases in department budgets, 2009 to 2016

B. Growth of Federal Debt and its Relationship to the Gross Domestic Product (GDP)

C. World Events and the Growth of the Federal Debt

D. Glossary

APPENDIX A

Percentage increases in department budgets, 2009 to 2016

Annual percentage increases (decreases) in budgeted expenditures

Agency or Branch	2009	2010	2011	2012	2013	2014	2015	2016
Executive Branch	(37%)	(22%)	(20%)	24%	(3%)	(2%)	0%	2%
Legislative Branch	7%	24%	(16%)	8%	(3%)	(3%)	(1%)	2%
Judicial Branch	5%	8%	3%	3%	(4%)	2%	1%	2%
Dept. of Defense (War)	7%	5%	11%	(4%)	(8%)	(2%)	1%	1%
Dept. of the Treasury	28%	(37%)	20%	6%	10%	17%	15%	11%
Dept. of Justice	4%	7%	13%	(1%)	1%	(4%)	(1%)	7%
Dept. of State	22%	11%	21%	12%	(2%)	(4%)	(4%)	0%
Dept. of Agriculture	26%	13%	17%	5%	1%	(6%)	(6%)	(2%)
Dept. of Interior	20%	12%	(1%)	6%	(8%)	(4%)	(2%)	1%
Dept. of Commerce	39%	23%	(10%)	11%	(16%)	(3%)	0%	2%
Dept. of Labor	135%	25%	(14%)	(26%)	(24%)	(8%)	(6%)	(3%)
Dept. of Health and Human Services	14%	7%	7%	(2%)	6%	14%	7%	8%
Dept. of Veterans Affairs	13%	13%	30%	(12%)	8%	6%	5%	9%
Dept. of Housing and Urban Dev.	24%	(1%)	1%	(19%)	(8%)	(4%)	(4%)	(1%)
Dept. of Transportation	12%	7%	2%	13%	6%	3%	2%	3%
Dept. of Energy	11%	30%	45%	(7%)	(16%)	(10%)	(3%)	(6%)
Dept. of Education	(19%)	74%	(15%)	(11%)	(5%)	4%	8%	7%
Environmental Protection Agency	2%	36%	1%	(10%)	(27%)	1%	4%	3%
Dept. of Homeland Security	27%	(14%)	8%	(2%)	(3%)	(3%)	3%	3%

APPENDIX B

Growth of Federal Debt and its Relationship to the Gross Domestic Product (GDP)

"For most countries, exceeding a debt-to-GDP ratio of 77% is a serious concern, according to the World Bank. However, the United States is hovering at a 100% debt-to-GDP ratio, without any apparent ill effects. Investors continue to purchase Treasury bills, notes, and bonds, keeping interest rates down. They know the U.S. government, and the Federal Reserve, won't allow the country to default."

"On the other hand, such a large debt-to-GDP ratio threatens the economy like the undersea portion of an iceberg. Just knowing it is there is enough to keep the economic engine from running at full throttle."

Kimberly Amadeo
President, WorldMoneyWatch.com

Author of the Ultimate Obamacare Handbook (Fall 2015) and Beyond the Great Recession
U.S. Economy Expert for About.com

History of the Federal Budget, Federal Debt, and GDP
Danger Zone > 80%GDP

Year	President	Party	Surplus	Debt	% Change	GDP	% Change	Debt/ GDP
1929	Hoover	Republican	734	16,931		1,060,000		2%
1930	Hoover	Republican	738	16,185	-4%	970,000	-8%	2%
1931	Hoover	Republican	-462	16,801	4%	900,000	-7%	2%
1932	Hoover	Republican	-2,735	19,487	16%	790,000	-12%	2%
1933	FDR	Democrat	-3,586	27,053	39%	780,000	-1%	3%
1934	FDR	Democrat	-3,586	27,053	0%	860,000	10%	3%
1935	FDR	Democrat	-2,803	28,701	6%	940,000	9%	3%
1936	FDR	Democrat	-4,304	33,779	18%	1,060,000	13%	3%
1937	FDR	Democrat	-2,193	36,425	8%	1,100,000	4%	3%
1938	FDR	Democrat	-89	37,165	2%	1,080,000	-2%	3%
1939	FDR	Democrat	-2,846	40,440	9%	1,160,000	7%	3%
1940	FDR	Democrat	-2,920	42,968	6%	1,270,000	9%	3%
1941	FDR	Democrat	-4,941	48,961	14%	1,490,000	17%	3%
1942	FDR	Democrat	-20,503	72,422	48%	1,770,000	19%	4%
1943	FDR	Democrat	-54,554	136,696	89%	2,070,000	17%	7%
1944	FDR	Democrat	-47,557	201,003	47%	2,240,000	8%	9%
1945	Truman	Democrat	-15,936	258,682	29%	2,220,000	-1%	12%
1946	Truman	Democrat	4,018	269,422	4%	1,960,000	-12%	14%
1947	Truman	Democrat	11,796	258,286	-2%	1,960,000	0%	13%
1948	Truman	Democrat	580	252,292	-2%	2,040,000	4%	12%
1949	Truman	Democrat	-3,119	252,770	0%	2,000,000	-2%	13%
1950	Truman	Democrat	-3,119	257,357	2%	2,270,000	14%	11%
1951	Truman	Democrat	6,102	255,222	-1%	2,400,000	6%	11%
1952	Truman	Democrat	-1,519	259,105	2%	2,530,000	5%	10%
1953	Eisenhower	Republican	-6,493	266,071	3%	2,540,000	0%	10%
1954	Eisenhower	Republican	-1,154	271,260	2%	2,610,000	3%	10%

Year	President	Party	Surplus	Debt	% Change	GDP	% Change	Debt/ GDP
1955	Eisenhower	Republican	-2,993	274,374	1%	2,780,000	7%	10%
1956	Eisenhower	Republican	3,947	272,751	-1%	2,840,000	2%	10%
1957	Eisenhower	Republican	3,412	270,527	-1%	2,850,000	0%	9%
1958	Eisenhower	Republican	-2,769	276,343	2%	2,920,000	2%	9%
1959	Eisenhower	Republican	-12,849	284,706	3%	3,060,000	5%	9%
1960	Eisenhower	Republican	301	286,331	1%	3,780,000	24%	8%
1961	JFK	Democrat	-3,335	288,971	1%	3,280,000	-13%	9%
1962	JFK	Democrat	-7,146	305,860	6%	3,420,000	4%	9%
1963	JFK/LBJ	Democrat	-4,756	305,860	0%	3,060,000	-11%	10%
1964	LBJ	Democrat	-5,915	311,713	2%	3,780,000	24%	8%
1965	LBJ	Democrat	-1,411	317,274	2%	4,100,000	8%	8%
1966	LBJ	Democrat	-3,698	319,907	1%	4,290,000	5%	7%
1967	LBJ	Democrat	-8,643	326,221	2%	4,400,000	3%	7%
1968	LBJ	Democrat	-25,161	347,578	7%	4,620,000	5%	8%
1969	Nixon	Republican	3,242	353,720	2%	4,720,000	2%	7%
1970	Nixon	Republican	-2,842	370,919	5%	4,710,000	0%	8%
1971	Nixon	Republican	-23,033	398,130	7%	4,910,000	4%	8%
1972	Nixon	Republican	-23,373	427,261	7%	5,250,000	7%	8%
1973	Nixon	Republican	-14,908	458,142	7%	5,460,000	4%	8%
1974	Nixon/For d	Republican	-6,135	475,060	4%	5,360,000	-2%	9%
1975	Ford	Republican	-53,242	533,189	12%	5,490,000	2%	10%
1976	Ford	Republican	-73,732	620,433	16%	5,730,000	4%	11%
1977	Carter	Democrat	-53659	698,840	13%	6,020,000	5%	12%
1978	Carter	Democrat	-59,185	771,544	10%	6,420,000	7%	12%
1979	Carter	Democrat	-40,726	826,519	7%	6,500,000	1%	13%
1980	Carter	Democrat	-73,830	907,701	10%	6,500,000	0%	14%
1981	Reagan	Republican	-78,968	997,855	10%	6,590,000	1%	15%

Year	President	Party	Surplus	Debt	% Change	GDP	% Change	Debt/ GDP
1982	Reagan	Republican	-127,977	1,142,034	14%	6,490,000	-2%	18%
1983	Reagan	Republican	-207,802	1,377,210	21%	7,000,000	8%	20%
1984	Reagan	Republican	-185,637	1,572,266	14%	7,400,000	6%	21%
1985	Reagan	Republican	-212,308	1,823,103	16%	7,710,000	4%	24%
1986	Reagan	Republican	-221,277	2,125,303	17%	7,940,000	3%	27%
1987	Reagan	Republican	-149,730	2,350,277	11%	8,290,000	4%	28%
1988	Reagan	Republican	-155,178	2,602,338	11%	8,610,000	4%	30%
1989	GHWB	Republican	-152,639	2,857,431	10%	8,850,000	3%	32%
1990	GHWB	Republican	-221,036	3,233,314	13%	8,910,000	1%	36%
1991	GHWB	Republican	-269,238	3,665,303	13%	9,020,000	1%	41%
1992	GHWB	Republican	-290,321	4,064,621	11%	9,410,000	4%	43%
1993	Clinton	Democrat	-255,051	4,411,489	9%	9,650,000	3%	46%
1994	Clinton	Democrat	-203,186	4,692,750	6%	10,050,000	4%	47%
1995	Clinton	Democrat	-163,952	4,973,983	6%	10,280,000	2%	48%
1996	Clinton	Democrat	-107,431	5,224,811	5%	10,704,000	4%	49%
1997	Clinton	Democrat	-21,884	5,413,146	4%	11,210,000	5%	48%
1998	Clinton	Democrat	69,270	5,526,193	2%	11,770,000	5%	47%
1999	Clinton	Democrat	125,610	5,656,271	2%	12,320,000	5%	46%
2000	Clinton	Democrat	236,241	5,674,178	0%	12,680,000	3%	45%
2001	GWB	Republican	128,236	5,807,463	2%	12,710,000	0%	46%
2002	GWB	Republican	-157,758	6,228,236	7%	12,960,000	2%	48%
2003	GWB	Republican	-377,585	6,783,231	9%	13,530,000	4%	50%
2004	GWB	Republican	-412,727	7,379,053	9%	13,950,000	3%	53%
2005	GWB	Republican	-318,346	7,932,710	8%	14,370,000	3%	55%

Year	President	Party	Surplus	Debt	% Change	GDP	% Change	Debt/ GDP
2006	GWB	Republican	-248,181	8,506,974	7%	14,720,000	2%	58%
2007	GWB	Republican	-160,701	9,007,653	6%	14,940,000	1%	60%
2008	GWB	Republican	-458,553	10,024,725	11%	14,580,000	-2%	69%
2009	BHO	Democrat	-1,412,688	11,909,829	19%	14,540,000	0%	82%
2010	BHO	Democrat	-1,294,373	13,561,623	14%	15,920,000	9%	85%
2011	BHO	Democrat	-1,299,593	14,790,340	9%	15,190,000	-5%	97%
2012	BHO	Democrat	-1,086,963	16,066,241	9%	15,430,000	2%	104%
2013	BHO	Democrat	-972,902	17,039,143	6%	15,920,000	3%	107%
2014	BHO	Democrat	-744,189	17,783,332	4%	16,160,000	2%	110%
2015	BHO	Democrat	-576,472	18,359,804	3%	18,537,000	15%	99%

APPENDIX C

World Events and the Growth of the Federal Debt

World Events		Federal Debt	Gross Domestic Product	Debt/GDP (Debt/Equity)	Danger Zone ≥80%
Hitler	1926	19,643,216,315			
Hitler	1927	18,511,906,932			
Hitler	1928	17,604,293,201			
Stock Market Crash	1929	16,931,088,484	1,060,000,000,000	2%	
The Great Depression	1930	16,185,309,831	970,000,000,000	2%	
The Great Depression	1931	16,801,281,492	900,000,000,000	2%	
The Great Depression	1932	19,487,002,444	790,000,000,000	2%	
The Great Depression	1933	22,538,672,560	780,000,000,000	3%	
The Great Depression	1934	27,053,141,414	860,000,000,000	3%	
The Great Depression	1935	28,700,892,625	940,000,000,000	3%	
The Great Depression	1936	33,778,543,494	1,060,000,000,000	3%	
The Great Depression	1937	36,424,613,732	1,110,000,000,000	3%	
The Great Depression	1938	37,164,740,315	1,080,000,000,000	3%	
The Great Depression	1939	40,439,532,411	1,160,000,000,000	3%	
Battle of Britain	1940	42,967,531,038	1,270,000,000,000	3%	
Pearl Harbor	1941	48,961,443,536	1,490,000,000,000	3%	
Bataan Death March	1942	72,422,445,116	1,770,000,000,000	4%	
Italy joins Allies	1943	136,696,090,330	2,070,000,000,000	7%	
D-Day	1944	201,003,387,221	2,240,000,000,000	9%	

Germany surrenders	1945	258,682,187,410	2,220,000,000,000	12%	
Nuremberg trials	1946	269,422,099,173	1,960,000,000,000	14%	
Marshall Plan	1947	258,286,383,109	1,960,000,000,000	13%	
Israel founded	1948	252,292,246,513	2,040,000,000,000	12%	
NATO established	1949	252,770,359,860	2,000,000,000,000	13%	
Korean War begins	1950	257,357,352,351	2,270,000,000,000	11%	
Treaty with Japan	1951	255,221,976,815	2,400,000,000,000	11%	
Polio vaccines	1952	259,105,178,785	2,530,000,000,000	10%	
Stalin dies	1953	266,071,061,639	2,540,000,000,000	10%	
Segregation illegal	1954	271,259,599,108	2,610,000,000,000	10%	
Warsaw pact	1955	274,374,222,803	2,780,000,000,000	10%	
Hungarian revolution	1956	272,750,813,649	2,840,000,000,000	10%	
Russian Sputnik	1957	270,527,171,896	2,850,000,000,000	9%	
NASA founded	1958	276,343,217,746	2,920,000,000,000	9%	
Castro dictator of Cuba	1959	284,705,907,078	3,060,000,000,000	9%	
WORLD EVENTS		FEDERAL DEBT	GDP	DEBT GDP	
First televised Presidential debates	1960	286,330,760,848	3,080,000,000,000	9%	
Bay of Pigs invasion	1961	288,970,938,610	3,280,000,000,000	9%	
Cuban missile crisis	1962	298,200,822,721	3,420,000,000,000	9%	
JFK assassinated	1963	305,859,632,996	3,060,000,000,000	10%	
Civil Rights Act	1964	311,712,899,257	3,780,000,000,000	8%	
US troops to Vietnam	1965	317,273,898,984	4,100,000,000,000	8%	
Black Panther party	1966	319,907,087,795	4,290,000,000,000	7%	
First heart transplant	1967	326,220,937,795	4,400,000,000,000	7%	
MLK and RFK assassinated	1968	347,578,406,426	4,620,000,000,000	8%	

First man on the moon	1969	353,720,253,841	4,720,000,000,000	7%	
Palestinians highjack planes	1970	370,918,706,950	4,710,000,000,000	8%	
VCRs introduced	1971	398,129,744,456	4,910,000,000,000	8%	
Terrorists attack Olympics	1972	427,260,460,941	5,250,000,000,000	8%	
Roe v Wade	1973	458,141,605,312	5,460,000,000,000	8%	
Nixon resigns	1974	475,059,815,732	5,360,000,000,000	9%	
Microsoft founded	1975	533,189,000,000	5,490,000,000,000	10%	
First Ebola outbreak	1976	620,433,000,000	5,730,000,000,000	11%	
Elvis found dead	1977	698,840,000,000	6,020,000,000,000	12%	
Jonestown massacre	1978	771,544,000,000	6,420,000,000,000	12%	
Iran takes American hostages	1979	826,519,000,000	6,500,000,000,000	13%	
John Lennon assassinated	1980	907,701,000,000	6,500,000,000,000	14%	
AIDS begins	1981	997,855,000,000	6,590,000,000,000	15%	
Argentina invades Falkan Islands	1982	1,142,034,000,000	6,490,000,000,000	18%	
Sally Ride, first woman in space	1983	1,377,210,000,000	7,000,000,000,000	20%	
Indira Gandhi killed	1984	1,572,266,000,000	7,400,000,000,000	21%	
Wreck of Titanic found	1985	1,823,103,000,000	7,710,000,000,000	24%	
Challenger explodes	1986	2,125,302,616,658	7,940,000,000,000	27%	
Black Monday	1987	2,350,276,890,953	8,290,000,000,000	28%	
US shoots down Iranian airliner	1988	2,602,337,712,041	8,610,000,000,000	30%	
Berlin Wall falls	1989	2,857,430,960,187	8,850,000,000,000	32%	
US invades Nicaragua	1990	3,233,313,451,777	8,910,000,000,000	36%	
Collapse of the Soviet Union	1991	3,665,303,351,697	9,020,000,000,000	41%	
Official end of the Cold War	1992	4,064,620,655,522	9,410,000,000,000	43%	

WORLD EVENTS		FEDERAL DEBT	GDP	DEBT GDP	DANGER ZONE
World Trade Center bombed	1993	4,411,488,883,139	9,650,000,000,000	46%	
Rwandan genocide	1994	4,692,749,910,013	10,050,000,000,000	47%	
Oklahoma City bombing	1995	4,973,982,900,709	10,280,000,000,000	48%	
Mad Cow disease in Britain	1996	5,224,810,939,136	10,704,000,000,000	49%	
Princess Diana dies in car crash	1997	5,413,146,011,397	11,210,000,000,000	48%	
Clinton Impeached	1998	5,526,193,008,898	11,770,000,000,000	47%	
Killing spree at Columbine	1999	5,656,270,901,615	12,320,000,000,000	46%	
USS Cole bombed	2000	5,674,178,209,887	12,680,000,000,000	45%	
Twin Towers destroyed	2001	5,807,463,412,200	12,710,000,000,000	46%	
Terrorists attack in Indonesia	2002	6,228,235,965,597	12,960,000,000,000	48%	
Invasion of Iraq	2003	6,783,231,062,744	13,530,000,000,000	50%	
Train bombings in Madrid	2004	7,379,052,696,330	13,950,000,000,000	53%	
Hurricane Katrina	2005	7,932,709,661,724	14,370,000,000,000	55%	
Saddam Hussein is executed	2006	8,506,973,899,215	14,720,000,000,000	58%	
Suicide bombings in Iraq	2007	9,007,653,372,262	14,990,000,000,000	60%	
Cyclone devastates Burma	2008	10,024,724,896,912	14,580,000,000,000	69%	
Major breakthrough in cancer research	2009	11,909,829,003,512	14,540,000,000,000	82%	80%
Earthquake in Haiti	2010	13,561,623,030,892	14,940,000,000,000	91%	80%
Japan devastated by earthquake	2011	14,790,340,328,557	15,190,000,000,000	97%	80%
Mayan calendar ends	2012	16,066,241,407,386	15,430,000,000,000	104%	80%
China's first unmanned moon landing	2013	16,738,183,526,697	15,920,000,000,000	105%	80%

Trade Center rebuilt	2014	17,824,071,380,734	16,160,000,000,000	110%	80%

APPENDIX D

Glossary

Glossary

BEA: Bureau of Economic Analysis's national economic program provides a quantitative view of US domestic production, consumption, and investment, of exports and imports, and of national and domestic income and saving. (www.bea.gov)

Constitutional Budget: A federal budget using the departments identified in the U.S. Constitution based on the author's interpretation.

FASAB: Federal Accounting Standards Advisory Board. The FASAB serves the public interest by improving federal financial reporting through issuing federal financial accounting standards and providing guidance after considering the needs of external and internal users of federal financial information. (www.fasab.gov)

FASB: Since 1973, the Financial Accounting Standards Board has been the designated organization in the private sector for establishing standards of financial accounting that governs the preparation of financial reports by nongovernmental organizations. (www.fasb.org)

Federal Debt: The Debt Held by the Public is all federal debt held by individuals, corporations, state or local governments, Federal Reserve Banks, foreign investments, and other entities outside the United States Government less Federal Financing Bank securities. Types of securities held by the public include, but are not limited to, Treasury Bills, Notes, Bonds, TIPS, United States Savings Bonds, and State and Local Government Series securities. Federal Debt also includes intragovernmental holdings that are held by Government trust funds, revolving funds, and special funds, and Federal Financing Bank securities. A small amount of marketable securities are held by government accounts. (www.investopedia.com)

Financing Activities: As defined for this Statement of Cash Flow, financing activities include transactions of principal and interest on the federal debt.

Free Cash Flow: As defined for this Statement of Cash Flow, free cash flow is the amount of cash available for payment of principal and interest on the federal debt after covering operating expenditures (operating activities) and capital investments (investing activities).

GAAP: Generally Accepted Accounting Principles are the guidelines that govern financial reporting as promulgated by the Financial Accounting Foundation.

GDP: Gross Domestic Product is the monetary value of all the finished goods and services produced within a country's borders in a specific time period, though GDP is usually calculated on an annual basis. It includes all of the private and public consumption, government outlays, investments, and exports less imports that occur within a defined territory. (www.investopedia.com)

Investing Activities: As defined for this Statement of Cash Flow, investing activities are expenditures for long-lived assets such as federal highways, the space programs, federal housing, and other similar expenditures.

Operating Activities: As defined for this Statement of Cash Flow, operating activities are expenditures within each department for normal expenses incurred to accomplish each department's mission statement.

SFFAS: Statements of Federal Financial Accounting Standards that are authoritative documents resulting from Federal Accounting Standards Advisory Board (FASAB) processes.

Statement of Cash Flow: As defined for this Statement of Cash Flow, the Statement presents tax revenues less expenditures for operating activities, investing activities, and financing activities. The resulting cash flow (positive or negative) represents the federal budget surplus or deficit. If the resulting cash flow is positive, it is presumed the excess cash will be used to pay principal on the federal debt. If the resulting cash flow is negative, it is presumed the deficit will be covered by additional borrowings on the federal debt.

Statement of Changes in Cash Balance: The primary purpose of this statement is to report how the annual unified budget deficit relates to the change in the Government's cash and other monetary assets and debt held by the public. It explains why the unified budget deficit normally would not result in an equivalent change in the Government's cash and other monetary assets. (www.fms.treas.gov)

Transparency: Transparency promotes accountability and provides information for citizens about what their Government is doing. Information *maintained by the Federal Government is a national asset. My Administration will take appropriate action, consistent with law and* policy, to disclose information rapidly in forms that the public can readily find and use. Executive departments and bureaus should harness new technologies to put information about their operations and decisions online and readily available to the public. Executive departments and bureaus should also solicit public feedback to identify information of greatest use to the public. (http://www.whitehouse.gov/the_press_office/TransparencyandOpenGover nment).

Understanding: The quality or condition of one who understands; comprehension. The faculty by which one understands; intelligence.

(http://www.thefreedictionary.com/understanding).

Undistributed offsetting receipts: Offsetting receipts that are deducted from the government-wide totals for budget authority and outlays instead of offset against a specific agency and function.

(www.taxpolicycenter.org)

REFERENCES

References

Bureau of Economic Activity (2015). *Who we are.* http://www.bea.gov/about

Department of Agriculture (2015). *About USDA – A Quick Reference Guide.* http://www.usda.gov

Department of Defense (2015). *About the Department of Defense.* http://defense.gov

Department of Energy (2015). *Office of Information Resources.* http://energy.gov

Department of Health and Human Services (2015). *About HHS.* http://www.hhs.gov

Department of Homeland Security (2015). *About DHS.* http://www.dhs.gov

Department of Housing and Urban Development (2015). *About HUD.* Portal.hud.gov/hudportal/HUD

Department of Justice (2015). *About DOJ.* http://www.justice.gov

Department of Labor (2015). *About the U.S. Department of Labor.* http://www.dol.gov

Department of State (2015). *About State.* http://www.state.gov

Department of the Interior (2015). *Who we are.*

http://www.doi.gov

Department of Transportation (2015). *About DOT.*
http://www.transportation.gov

Department of Treasury (2015). *About.*
http://www.treasury.gov

Environmental Protection Agency (2015). *About EPA.*
http://www.epa.gov

Kids Law (2015). *Understanding the Preamble.*
Kids.law.com/preamble-of-the-constitution

Legislative Branch (2015). *The Legislative Branch.*
https://www.whitehouse.gov/1600/legislative-branch

Office of Personnel Management (2015). *Our Agency.*
http://www.opm.gov

Social Security Administration (2015). *About the Social Security Administration.*
http://www.ssa.gov

ADDITIONAL BIBLIOGRAPHY

Bibliography

Archives.gov (2015). *The Charters of Freedom. Constitution of the United States.*
http://www.archives.gov/exhibits/charters/constitution.html

Beacon Learning Center (2015). *The Meaning of the Preamble of the United States.*
www.beaconlearningcenter.com/documents/5215_4498.pdf

Billofrightsinstitute.org. *Educating Young People about the Constitution.*
http:billofrightsinstitute.org

Constitution Center (2015). *The Preamble.*
http://constitutioncenter.org/constitution/preamble/preamble

Constitution for Kids (2015). *Preamble to the United States Constitution.*
http://const4kids.forums.commonground13.us/?p=19

Dummies.com (2015). *The 7 Articles of the US Constitution.*

http://www.dummies.com/how-to/content/the-7-articles-of-the-constitution.html

Education Portal (2015). *The Preamble to the Constitution: Definition, Summary, Purpose & Examples.* http://education-portal.com/academy/lesson/the-preamble-to-the-constitution-definition-summary-purpose-examples.html

Heritage.org (2015). *The Heritage Guide to the Constitution: Fully Revised Second Edition.*
http://www.heritage.org/constitution#!/articles/0/essays/1/preamble

Home School Pool (2015). *Home School Explanation of the Preamble.* http://homeschoolpool.info/home_school_cirriculum/home-school-government/home-school-explanation-of-the-preamble

Kids Laws (2015). *What is the Preamble?* http://kids.laws.com/preamble-of-the-constitution

National Priorities.org. *Budget Process. Who decides the Federal Budget?.* https://www.nationalpriorities.org/budget-basics/federal-budget-101/federal-budget-process/

Oxford Journals (2015). *The preamble in constitutional interpretation.* http://icon.oxfordjournals.org/content/8/4/714.abstract

Quizlet (2015). *7 Articles of the Constitution.* http://quizlet.com/7979990-7-articles-of-the-constitution-flash-cards/

Republican National Committee. *We the People: A Restoration of Constitutional Government.* https://www.gop.com/platform/we-the-people/

Scholastic.com (2015). *The Articles of the Constitution.* http://www.scholastic.com/browse/article.jsp?id=7466

Taxpolicycenter.org. *Declaration of Independence* http://archives.gov/exhibits/charters/declaration.html

The Concord Coalition. *First Budget.* http://www.concordcoalition.org/issues/federal-budget-0

WATCHDOG ORGANIZATIONS

Citizens Against Government Waste. (cagw.org)

Citizens for Responsibility and Ethics in Washington. (www.citizensforethics.org)

Common Cause. (www.commoncause.org)

First Budget. (firstbudget.org)

Fix the Debt. (www.fixthedebt.org)

Flip the Debt. (www.flipthedebt.org)

Judicial Watch. (www.judicialwatch.org)

Peter G. Peterson Foundation. (pgpf.org)

Politico. (www.politico.org)

ProPublica. (www.propublica.org)

The Center for Media and Democracy. (www.sourcewatch.org)

The Concord Coalition. (www.concordcoalition.org)

The Heritage Foundation. (opportunity.heritage.org)

POST SCRIPT

On June 25, 2015, the Supreme Court of the United States (SCOTUS) voted 6-3 to uphold the 'exchange' provision in The Patient Protection and Affordable Care Act (ACA).

Voting in favor of upholding the Act were Justices Kennedy, Ginsburg, Breyer, Sotomayor, Kagan, and Chief Justice Roberts. Voting against were Justices Scalia, Thomas, and Alito.

The ACA was modeled after the Massachusetts health system and adopted a version of the three key reforms that made the Massachusetts system successful. First, the Act adopts the guaranteed issue and community rating requirements. Second, the Act generally requires individuals to maintain health insurance coverage or make a payment to the IRS, unless the cost of buying insurance would exceed eight percent of that individual's income. Third, the Act seeks to make insurance more affordable by giving refundable tax credits to individuals with household income between 100 percent and 400 percent of the federal poverty line.

In addition, the Act requires the creation of an 'Exchange' in each State-basically, a marketplace that allows people to compare and purchase insurance plans. The Act gives each State the opportunity to establish its own Exchange but provides that the Federal Government will establish 'such Exchange' if the State does not.

Their decision, in part, stated 'the combination of no tax credits and an ineffective coverage requirement could well push a State's individual insurance market into a death spiral'. 'It is implausible that Congress meant the Act to operate in this manner. Congress made the guaranteed issue and community rating requirements applicable in every State in the Nation, but those requirements only work when combined with the coverage requirement and tax credits.' 'It thus stands to reason that Congress meant for those provisions to apply in every State as well'. (Supreme Court of the United States, No. 14-114. Decided June 25, 2015)

Currently there are 22 States without a State Exchange. Cost estimates will have to be revised in light of this court decision. Whatever the cost, the federal debt will most likely increase as a result of adding the additional States.

The decision was apparently based on 'intent' rather than the letter of the law.

ABOUT THE AUTHOR

Dale is a CPA (1974), has a BS in Accounting, an MBA in Health Services Management, and a DBA in Accounting (2014). He is married with three adult children, five grandchildren, and one great-grandson. His wife, Linda, has two adult children and three grandchildren.

He is an adjunct professor, teaching accounting and finance for several Arkansas colleges and is a substitute teacher for K-12.

He is a native of Arkansas and served in the US Navy from 1962 to 1968 including two years active duty.

Printed by Libri Plureos GmbH in Hamburg,
Germany